"*Soul Journey* is a sacred invitation to encounter God's presence woven through our lives. Dr. Barbara Peacock offers grace, wisdom, and a life-giving guide I wholeheartedly recommend to every reader."

—**Dr. Michelle Boone-Thornton**,
World Civility Ambassador

"*Soul Journey* is a powerful invitation to deeper spiritual reflection and growth. Barbara Peacock writes with authenticity, wisdom, and a deep care for the reader's soul. A truly meaningful guide for anyone seeking spiritual renewal."

—**Rev. Dr. C. Lynn Brinkley**

"Dr. Peacock aptly challenges readers to explore how their lived experiences are a profound site for examining both God's presence and purposeful formation through reflection, prayer, and writing. This process will undoubtedly provide readers with restoration, direction, and a renewed sense of purpose."

—**Nadia E. Brown**, professor of government
and chair of Women's and Gender Studies
Program, Georgetown University

"In *Soul Journey*, Dr. Barbara Peacock offers a deeply personal and theologically rich introduction to the practice of writing one's spiritual autobiography. Filled with stories and reflective prompts, this easy-to-read book will be of interest to anyone seeking to discern God's presence in the various dimensions of their life story. A wonderful resource!"

—**E. Trey Clark**, assistant professor of preaching
and spiritual formation, Fuller Theological Seminary

"If you're seeking to bring your walk with God into sharper focus, this book offers meaningful insight, encouragement, application, and clarity. It's not just a read—it's a spiritual invitation."

— **Dr. Adrienne Garabedian**, assistant vice provost
and program dean, Strayer University

"Biblically rich and filled with pastoral encouragement, deep wisdom, practical exercises, and others' witness, *Soul Journey* will help you recognize God in your own story as God continues to write the story of your life."

—**Rev. Bill Haley**, executive director, Coracle

"In *Soul Journey*, Dr. Peacock has given a profound gift to the ongoing adventure of spiritual formation. Her penchant for carefully, powerfully, and slowly mining the rich resources of spiritual tradition for deep formation are evident throughout this work. Given the words of Irenaeus, that the glory of God is a fully alive human being, anyone who walks through this faithful guide will certainly be on the journey of all souls: to become more fully alive in the deep love of God."

—**Rev. Dr. Preston M. Hill**, assistant professor of Integrative Theology, Richmont Graduate University

"Dr. Barbara Peacock is on to something! Following Jesus requires story work. In *Soul Journey* Barbara takes readers on an expedition of reflection. If you write your story with her, you'll have clarity and power to bend your future in the direction of Jesus."

—**Bishop Todd Hunter**, author of *What Jesus Intended*

"In *Soul Journey*, Dr. Barbara Peacock takes you on a biblically rooted pilgrimage into your past, uncovering the barriers that keep you from deeper spiritual formation today. Barbara has a unique gift of getting to the core. I've personally experienced this in my own journey and the lives of our leaders as they wrote their spiritual autobiographies with her guidance. This book is a treasure for anyone longing for true spiritual transformation."

—**Rob Kelly**, founder and CEO, For Charlotte Network; cofounder and CEO, City Leaders Collective

"Enter your soul journey prayerfully and reflectively, record the gifts of remembrance, and be sure to say thank you to the One who gives you life. This book is an important reminder."

—**Stephen A. Macchia**, founder and president, Leadership Transformations; author of 17 books

"This book will help the blind mindset to see and the captive heart to be free as they journey into their past and, ultimately, find beloved transformation."

—**Debbie Manigat**, DMFT, LMFT, spiritual director

"In *Soul Journey*, Dr. Peacock writes with the wisdom and depth that come from years of leading others in spiritual formation and direction. Her voice is trustworthy, her heart is genuine, and her insights invite us to encounter God with fresh clarity and hope."

—**Nicole Massie Martin**, author of *Nailing It: Why Successful Leadership Demands Suffering and Surrender*

"It is a pleasure to endorse the latest book from my friend and colleague, Barbara Peacock. *Soul Journey* is a delightful resource for learning how to get the most from writing a personal spiritual autobiography, or, to use Ignatian language, the systematic Examine of a life."

—**Gary W. Moon**, MDiv, PhD, founding executive director,
Martin Institute, and Dallas Willard Center,
Westmont College, and Renovaré; author

"I know of no one who can guide others through their spiritual journey from past to present more deeply than the soul care guru, Barbara Peacock."

—**Tom Phillips**, senior advisor,
Billy Graham Evangelistic Association

"With the care of a pastor and skill and wisdom of a seasoned spiritual director, Dr. Peacock invites us to gently look back with grace and move forward with hope that our story is not random but woven into the tapestry of the Holy Spirit.

—**Tim Reist**, executive director, Space for Your Soul

"*Soul Journey* is steeped in a rich tradition of emotional wellness combined with decades of personal soul care experience. . . . This is a must-read and an ongoing resource to take you deeper in knowing the relationship between self and God."

—**Rev. Dr. J. Elvin Sadler**, general secretary-auditor,
The A.M.E. Zion Church; dean of doctoral studies,
United Theological Seminary

"High praise for *Soul Journey*, a wonderful invitation to take a long, loving look at your story where you find traces of the God-story woven throughout, at work shaping and forming you for His purposes. People are hurting and in pain. Storying ourselves through spiritual autobiography unlocks that pain, gives perspective, allows God to come close, and moves us toward healing. Written with clarity and depth, *Soul Journey* calls you into this exploration where you discover that you have always lived in the miracle of His story."

—**Dr. R. Neal Siler**, president and founder,
The Healing Place Center for Counseling
and Spiritual Formation, Mechanicsville, Virginia

SOUL JOURNEY

Transform Your Present by Rediscovering God in Your Past

BARBARA L. PEACOCK

Soul Journey: Transform Your Present by Rediscovering God in Your Past
© 2026 by Barbara L. Peacock

All rights reserved.

Requests for permission to quote from this book should be directed to: Permissions Department, Our Daily Bread Publishing, PO Box 3566, Grand Rapids, MI 49501; or contact us by email at permissionsdept@odbm.org.

Names have been used with permission.

Author is represented by the literary agency of Credo Communications LLC, Grand Rapids, Michigan, credocommunications.net.

Scripture quotations, unless otherwise indicated, are taken from the Holy Bible, New International Version®, NIV®. Copyright © 1973, 1978, 1984, 2011 by Biblica, Inc.™ Used by permission of Zondervan. All rights reserved worldwide. zondervan.com.

Scripture quotations marked ESV are taken from the ESV® Bible (The Holy Bible, English Standard Version®), copyright © 2001 by Crossway, a publishing ministry of Good News Publishers. Used by permission. All rights reserved.

Scripture quotations marked MSG are taken from *The Message*, copyright © 1993, 2002, 2018 by Eugene H. Peterson. Used by permission of NavPress. All rights reserved. Represented by Tyndale House Publishers.

Scripture quotations marked NKJV are taken from the New King James Version®. Copyright © 1982 by Thomas Nelson. Used by permission. All rights reserved.

Scripture quotations marked NRSV are taken from New Revised Standard Version, Updated Edition. Copyright © 2021 National Council of Churches of Christ in the United States of America. Used by permission. All rights reserved worldwide.

Interior design by Michael J. Williams

ISBN: 978-1-64070-454-1

Library of Congress Cataloging-in-Publication Data Available

Printed in the United States of America
26 27 28 29 30 31 32 33 / 8 7 6 5 4 3 2 1

CONTENTS

ACKNOWLEDGMENTS

Reading an enjoyable book is a treasure. Before enrolling and physically attending a class at Gordon-Conwell Theological Seminary, each student was required to read a book and do a book review. The book that I was assigned to read was about a young lady who was a French Carmelite. The book's title was *The Autobiography of Thérèse of Lisieux: The Story of a Soul.* When I received the assignment, it was challenging to wrap my mind around reading this unappealing book. The good news was I enjoyed my French classes at West Columbus High School (1969–1972) in Cerro Gordo, North Carolina and North Carolina Central University (1972–1976) in Durham, North Carolina.

Reading about a French girl who desired to be a Carmelite was far from the top of my list. Nonetheless, I dove into it, and much to my surprise, it became one of my favorite reads. Thérèse's sister encouraged her to write her journey. Likewise, my professors encouraged all students in the Doctor of Ministry program to write their spiritual autobiography.

Writing your spiritual autobiography was a prerequisite for all students pursuing the Doctor of Ministry in Spiritual Formation for Ministry Leaders at Gordon-Conwell Theological Seminary in 2004. Thank you, Dr. David Currie and Dr. Stephen Macchia, for your insight. This assignment changed how I look at discipleship, Christian education, and spiritual formation. Since I journeyed through the program, it has been on my heart to write a book about the spiritual autobiography. However, it has taken many years for me to have the chance to write about that topic and to pursue publication.

Prior to this book, God called me to write my first book entitled *CALLED to Teach*. (CALLED is an acronym for Commissioned As Leaders, Learners, Educators, and Disciples.) For this book, I was not a solo writer; several Christian educators in the Charlotte area committed to the compilation of this book. My next book was the award-winning book *Soul Care in African American Practice*. This book also has a workbook. After this book, I published two journals. The first was *Psalm 119 Scriptural Journal*, and the second was *He Restores My Soul: Psalm 23:3*. My most recent book is *Spiritual Practices for Soul Care: 40 Ways to Deepen Your Faith*. And now God has blessed me to write, *Soul Journey: Transform Your Present by Rediscovering God in Your Past*. This book is the culmination of over two decades of praying, teaching, writing, publishing, and seeking God for direction.

I have been tremendously blessed by all who have invested in my life with tender soul care. Thank you for your prayers, your support, and your spirit of faith. I am thankful for my family, colleagues, and friends, who have been extremely supportive. I am also thankful for those who felt it could not be done, but *God*!

To our pastor, Bishop Claude Richard Alexander Jr., and leading lady, Dr. Kimberly Nash Alexander, thanks for being the ultimate trailblazers. Your servant leadership is contagious. To the Park Church family, thank you for being who you are in the kingdom. You are the best congregation.

To the team at Barbara L. Peacock Ministries and Peacock Soul Care, thank you for your commitment to the journey. Many of you have shared in various ways. Consequently, the completion of this book has been accomplished. Always remember, I love you and pray God's abundant favor and blessings upon you and your household.

To my siblings, Darryl Lewis, Blondell Hester, and Tabitha Blue, thanks for your love and encouragement. To Vérnee Peacock Wilkinson, our lovely daughter, her wonderful husband, Michael Wilkinson, and our precious grandchildren, Eden and Eliah, thank you for your continuous support and care. I would especially like to thank God for Gilbert L. Peacock, my wonderful husband of forty-seven years. I am most appreciative and humbled by your generous love, encouraging words, prayers, cooking, and the numerous sacrifices you make. Your commitment to me and this journey made it possible for me to complete this book. I love you.

I praise God for His sustaining power that enabled me to finish this leg of the journey. To Him be the glory, forever and ever. Amen. Hallelujah.

INTRODUCTION

One of the most classic movies of the past century is *The Wizard of Oz*. In 1939, Metro-Goldwyn-Mayer produced this award-winning musical. In this movie based on a children's novel, Judy Garland plays the main character, teenager Dorothy Gale. In the screenplay, Dorothy gets caught up in a whirlwind and lands in an unknown space. Upon her arrival, her utmost dream is to return to her homeland, Kansas. Thus, she embarks upon a journey of twists and turns on the infamous yellow brick road. She meets several strangers who become her friends. What they all have in common is that they are all in need of a miracle. Together their goal is to see the Wizard, the only one who can grant them their heart's desire. Even though Dorothy feels lost on her journey, she never loses hope that she will return home. In this fictional story, the viewers travel with Dorothy and her friends in hopes that their dreams will come true.

The life journey you and I encounter is much like Dorothy's, even though her story is fictional and ours is very much real. We are all traveling on a road of twists and turns. Our prayer is that one day, we too will be blessed with experiencing the dream of our eternal home in a place called heaven. This is our eschatological hope.

Life is filled with ups and downs, highs and lows, and twists and turns. The journey with God is one filled with adventure and complexities that can often be overwhelming and incomprehensible. Yet, He is our traveling companion.[1] We never journey alone because He is forever with us, whether we acknowledge His presence or not.

Your Spiritual Autobiography

Through reading this book, my prayer is that you will learn to understand your spiritual journey better. Thus, I have committed to writing this book with a workbook in the back to guide you in documenting your story. I will describe some aspects of the spiritual autobiography, but the actual assignment of writing your spiritual autobiography will not occur until the end of the book. Once you write your spiritual autobiography, you will see patterns, a process, and a rhythm in which God has guided your life over the years.

A spiritual autobiography is an in-depth reflection of your journey with God. Writing about this journey calls you to look at the big picture and the intricacies, the exhilarating and the mundane, and the vague and the obvious moments of your finite life. Writing about your journey is not a time to be critical or proud, but a time to allow the pen or the keys on your apparatus to freely flow without inhibitions. This is not the time to become stuck and paralyzed in your reflections. It is a time to open your mind and your heart as you seek to see God's hand on your journey with Him. Sometimes this may seem like a roller-coaster ride, and sometimes it looks like nothing is happening. No matter how high you sense your journey has escalated, or how low the trials and tribulations of life have tried to detour and destroy your very soul, the good news is that God was there. You were never alone.

Implementing this sacred document is designed to equip

you to understand your unique journey. Understanding your journey better will cause a sense of calm within your very soul. Allow the various entities of your story to settle deep down within the crevices of your soul. Seek to embrace and accept the various vicissitudes—the ups and downs, highs and lows, good and bad times—of your journey. Please be mindful that some experiences will be more difficult to understand and accept than others. Prayerfully seek to understand them and to continue desiring to see God throughout your journey.

Understanding your story will help you to understand another person's story better as well. Once you can fully embrace your story, you will develop a sense of love for yourself. As a result, you will better understand your personal journey, and it will be easier for you to love your neighbor (Mark 12:31).

Writing your story is transformative and a life-changing spiritual discipline. The process of reflection, transparency, and discernment makes you a better disciple. Dissecting your journey is discipleship. When we are faithful disciples, we become faithful disciplers. And according to Jesus, making disciples is the greatest commission.[2]

Your spiritual autobiography is composed of you identifying significant events, people, and places that have influenced you on your soul journey. As you write about areas and benchmarks in your life, seek to discern the movement of God's hand and direction. Ask yourself questions like: Where was He, and what was He doing? During your writing, reflect on peaks and valleys—faith-filled and doubt-filled moments. During these reflective moments, listen to God's voice. What is He saying about all these moments?

In the process of your writing, it is imperative to be honest. Transparency with yourself is essential. This is a time to be willing to look at the good and the difficult parts of your journey. Truly, this is a time of vulnerability. While you are writing, be prayerful and do not allow the enemy to cause the spirit of guilt or shame to take root. Guilt and shame are enemies that may seek to creep in. Even though they may appear to be the same, they are different. Guilt informs you that you feel bad about yourself. Shame will tell you that *you* are bad. It is imperative not to allow either to dominate or control your thought process. Just keep moving forward in your writing when such thoughts try to dominate you.

Rediscovering God and Yourself

I am passionate about the implementation of this discipline because of the vast difference it makes in the lives of disciples. Far too often, individuals, members, and leaders in the faith community seek to serve in God's kingdom without fully understanding their own personal journey. Too much baggage and trauma have not been identified or dealt with, and thus, leaders are operating in the past. In pain. In deceit. In jealousy. In insecurity. In the false self. In burnout. In depression. In anxiety. Disciples of Christ are often stuck and do not know how to move forward. The lack of understanding ourselves affects how we see ourselves and impacts how we see others. Consequently, it affects how we serve in the faith community and in everyday life.

This book, *Soul Journey: Transform Your Present by Rediscovering God in Your Past*, is designed to get to the heart of the matter, which is connected to your personal and unique soul journey. As a result of your prayerful writing, the emerging wisdom, knowledge, and understanding of your journey will be evident and impactful.

In our current spiritual climate, the relevancy of the church is being reevaluated continuously. During such evaluation, I believe it is vital to implement the writing of one's spiritual autobiography in an effort to develop more mature disciples. *Soul Journey: Transform Your Present by Rediscovering God in Your Past* guides individuals to adhere to the principles of this ancient discipline with a fresh, innovative, relevant, and transformative approach.

During these critical times in the body of Christ, it is necessary for disciples of the Lord to better understand His ongoing activity in their lives. Many times, people are angry with God, confused about their purpose, and have become stuck and immobilized because of a lack of understanding of their spiritual journey. I pray that this book will be a metamorphic experience that will assist persons, churches, and organizations during the transformative process of connecting the dots of their journey, finding solace for their soul, and becoming more empowered for their journey.

This book is designed to help individuals to more effectively identify their true self and their false self. The true self is the most authentic version of oneself that aligns with God's unique character and gifting. The true self is a godly representation that exudes from the Holy Spirit within. The false self is a pretend self that seeks to camouflage the true self. The false self can play a dominant role in the life of an individual to the extent that the false self thinks it is the true self. By the grace of God, the false self can be demolished so that the true self can emerge, living out the best version of you.

Get Ready for the Deep Journey

For many of us, the act of writing about our personal journey is long overdue. Perhaps you have never considered it simply because no one ever introduced the idea. Or maybe someone did suggest it, but you dismissed it, setting it aside as unnecessary or too difficult to confront. I understand—gazing into the mirror of your life can be a daunting task. Yet, there is extraordinary value in doing so. Reflecting on the activity of God in your story is one of the most engaging, transformative, and empowering spiritual disciplines you can embrace. Truly, God's grace is sufficient and God ultimately desires that you allow Him to *Transform Your Present by Rediscovering God in Your Past.*

Beloved, you are not alone on this journey. The triune God—God the Father, God the Son, and God the Holy Spirit—walks with you each and every step of the way. There has never been a moment when the triune God was not there. God's divine presence is your guide, your comfort, and your strength. And I, too, will journey alongside you, offering insights and glimpses into my own spiritual walk—lessons learned, moments treasured, and truths discovered.

You may still find yourself asking, *Why is this deep dive calling me?* That is a profound and worthy question. I believe it is what some might describe as a "Jesus calling" moment. This is a sacred invitation to become a more discerning, faithful, and informed citizen of the kingdom of God. Ultimately, this is all for the glory of God and the fulfillment of the Spirit's purpose and plan for your life.

So take a deep breath. Open your heart, mind, and soul as you prepare to be amazed by what the Spirit will reveal. This is your sacred journey of remembrance, revelation, and renewal. Let's go . . . together.

Chapter 1

THE BEFORE

Whatever is has already been, and
what will be has been before; and
God will call the past to account.
Ecclesiastes 3:15

All the triune Godhead was in the beginning; God the Father, God the Son, and God the Holy Spirit are the authors of all of creation. The triune Godhead was in the beginning and is ever present. Before the Son of God ever set foot on the earth, He existed. He was before. In the book of Proverbs, the persona of Him as Wisdom is eloquently articulated.

> The Lord brought me forth as the first of
> his works,
> before his deeds of old;
> I was formed long ages ago,
> at the very beginning, when the world
> came to be.
> When there were no watery depths, I was
> given birth,
> when there were no springs overflowing
> with water;

before the mountains were settled in place,
before the hills, I was given birth,
before he made the world or its fields
or any of the dust of the earth.
I was there when he set the heavens in place,
when he marked out the horizon on the
face of the deep,
when he established the clouds above
and fixed securely the fountains of the
deep,
when he gave the sea its boundary
so the waters would not overstep his
command,
and when he marked out the foundations of
the earth.
Then I was constantly at his side.
I was filled with delight day after day,
rejoicing always in his presence,
rejoicing in his whole world
and delighting in mankind.
(Proverbs 8:22–31)

Theologically, this proverbial text correlates to the personhood of Jesus. He existed before the mountains and hills (Proverbs 8:25). He existed before the heavens were "in place." The presence of God the Son was in the beginning of time (Genesis 1:2).

> Then God said, "Let us make mankind in our image, in our likeness, so that they may rule over the fish in the sea and the birds in the sky, over the livestock and all the wild animals, and over all the creatures that move along the ground."

So God created mankind in his own image,
in the image of God he created them;
male and female he created them.
(Genesis 1:26–27)

The foreshadowing of Jesus, the Savior of the world, is a significant theme throughout the Old Testament. In Genesis 3, the author writes, "And I will put enmity between you and the woman, and between your offspring and hers; he will crush your head, and you will strike his heel" (v. 15). Jesus will crush the adversary's head. Another familiar passage that refers to the foreknowledge of Jesus is found in Isaiah 9: "For to us a child is born, to us a son is given, and the government will be on his shoulders. And he will be called Wonderful Counselor, Mighty God, Everlasting Father, Prince of Peace" (v. 6). These are just a few passages that speak to the "before" of Jesus. However, the Scripture references of Jesus in the Old Testament are far too many to share in a limited writing.

The triune God—God the Father, God the Son, and God the Holy Spirit—created humankind in the image and likeness of God's triune self. He created humanity in the *imago Dei*. He created humanity with purpose. He appointed and anointed humankind—male and female beings (Genesis 1:27)—to rule, and gave them dominion and authority over creation before He created them (Genesis 1:26).

Yahweh God is Alpha and Omega. He knows the end from the beginning. In His infinite mind, He planned to create everything that was, that is, and that is to come. At the beginning of time, He created everything. In five days, He created the sun, the moon, the stars, the plants, the trees, the fish, the fowl, and the animals. On the sixth day, He decided to make humanity in His image to complete the components of His creation.

Creation and Preformation

In Genesis 2, there is another account of creation: "Then the Lord God formed a man from the dust of the ground and breathed into his nostrils the breath of life, and the man became a living being" (v. 7).

The inception of the human race began when Yahweh God breathed into a shell of a man. God's breath and the dormant posture of man connected, and the man took on the form of life. God breathed His *ruach* (his breath of life) into the shell of a man, and man became a living soul; he became a living life, a living human being. Yahweh Elohim, the Creator of humanity, formed man out of the dry, loose dirt of the earth, and thus the inception of human life began!

Yahweh Elohim brought forth, birthed, molded, and manifested His divine desire for humanity into His reality and divine existence. Yahweh Elohim's innate desire for formation in His divine image was exhibited in the form of His human being. His announcement of this created human was that he was "very good."

The word *yatsar* is a powerful Hebrew term that reveals God's intimate and intentional act of creation. Found in passages like Genesis 2:7, *yatsar* is the verb used to describe how God "formed" humanity from the dust of the ground. This is not a distant or mechanical act—it is personal, deliberate, and full of divine care. *Yatsar* is the language of God's creative craftsmanship.

God's *yatsar* is not limited to the first breath of life given to Adam; it continues through generations, shaping and forming each of us uniquely. *Yatsar* is active in the formation of my life, in the shaping of your soul, and in the molding of all humanity. We are not mass-produced beings—we are fearfully and wonderfully *yatsar*-ed by the hands of the Creator.

This divine formation declares our identity as bearers of God's image—humanity that God called "very good." To embrace the work of *yatsar* is to recognize the sacredness of our becoming. It is to acknowledge that God's hands are still at work, forming our character, calling, and purpose according to His divine design.

The theme of preformation is found throughout the book of Genesis. In addition, this theme is articulated in the book of the major prophet, Jeremiah. When considering Yahweh Elohim's preformation, the prophet Jeremiah writes:

> The word of the LORD came to me, saying,
>
> "Before I formed you in the womb I knew
> you,
> before you were born I set you apart;
> I appointed you as a prophet to the
> nations."
>
> "Alas, Sovereign LORD," I said, "I do not know how to speak; I am too young."
>
> But the LORD said to me, "Do not say, 'I am too young.' You must go to everyone I send you to and say whatever I command you. Do not be afraid of them, for I am with you and will rescue you," declares the LORD.
>
> Then the LORD reached out his hand and touched my mouth and said to me, "I have put my words in your mouth. See, today I appoint you over nations and kingdoms to uproot and tear down, to destroy and overthrow, to build and to plant."
>
> The word of the LORD came to me: "What do you see, Jeremiah?"

> "I see the branch of an almond tree," I replied.
>
> The Lord said to me, "You have seen correctly, for I am watching to see that my word is fulfilled." (Jeremiah 1:4–12)

Awe! How this passage strikes the depths of my soul. God calls the prophet Jeremiah to travel with Him through God's *kairos* time (God's divine timing). God poignantly speaks to the prophet about his existence before the actual manifestation of his earthly birth.

In the passage, God speaks to Jeremiah about his before-birth time, God speaks to him about his current time, and God speaks to him about his future time. There is not a time that God is not present nor unaware of Jeremiah. All portions of Jeremiah's story are spoken of in the pericope[1] of time that is found in Jeremiah 1:4–12. God tells Jeremiah: "Before I formed you in the womb I knew you, before you were born I set you apart; I appointed you as a prophet to the nations" (Jeremiah 1:5). God assures Jeremiah of his current presence in verse 8 when He says, "I am with you," and in verse 10, "today I appoint you." God will be with Jeremiah in the future: "You must go to everyone I send you to and say whatever I command you . . . for I am with you and will rescue you" (v. 7–8), and in verse 12, "for I am watching to see that my word is fulfilled." Throughout the passage, there are ebbs and flows of God's past, present, and future presence with His prophet.

Likewise, God is with you at all times. He is never absent, even when you do not sense His holy presence. Let us look at some elements of your preformation and God's presence and kairos time in your life.

My dear sister and my dear brother, during your preformation, before your mother and father knew one another,

God knew you. Before you were conceived in the womb of your precious mother, God "set you apart."[2] This amazing fact is mind-boggling and beyond the comprehension of our finite minds. However, the truth remains. God preformed. God formed, He made, He designed, He created, He designated, and He consecrated you for His service, even before you were born or named. His preformation had a destination, to your formation, for your performance, all for His glorification.

Mr. James Weldon Johnson, a remarkable poet, penned a phenomenal interpretation of God's creation in his poem that is entitled "The Creation."[3] Johnson was born in Florida in 1871. He was a national organizer for the NAACP and an author of poetry and nonfiction. Even though he is best known for the song "Lift Every Voice and Sing," he is also well-known for his poetry. Take some time to read the beautiful words in "The Creation." You can find a copy easily online.

In this poem, James Weldon Johnson innately taps into the mind of God as he brilliantly pens God's heartfelt desire to live in a world with His creation. After God created the fish in the sea, the fowl in the air, and every living thing that creeps upon the face of the earth, he molded humanity in His image (Genesis 1–2).

God was fully complete within His God-self, but He chose to have a relationship with humanity. He had you in mind before anyone else had you on their radar. God intended for you to preexist. Let me say it this way: in the mind of God, you existed before you existed. I don't know about you, but that is mind-boggling for me. God has information about you and me that no one else on the planet has, not even the adversary. Your parents, public record, and AI are not privy to such heavenly knowledge, and neither are you and I.

The day you came forth into this world, you were named. Whether you were named by parents, grandparents, an auntie, an uncle, a cousin, a neighbor, or a friend, somebody took the time to name you. Most likely, you still go by that name or are called something similar to your birth name.

When you came into this world, God already had a plan in mind for you. Regardless of your personal sense of significance or lack thereof, Yahweh has an assignment just for you. He has something He created you to be and something He created you to do, that only you can be and only you can do. No one else has their name on your assignment. He put you on this earth with something specific in mind. I like to call it "the specificity of your assignment."

The enemy's strategic and calculated plan is to distract you from reaching your godly destiny. He desires to abort the manifestation of your full potential. He has deceptive lies to defer, distract, and deter you from fully seeking and accomplishing God's divine plan and purpose for your life. Such distractions and tactics that the enemy uses may include (but are not limited to):

- You do not know how to speak.
- The TOO's . . .
  - You are TOO young.
  - You are TOO old.
  - You are TOO sick.
  - You are TOO afraid.
  - You are TOO poor.
  - You are TOO rich.
  - You are TOO forgetful.
  - You are TOO dumb.
- You cannot do it.

- You are not enough.
- You do not need to do that.

Regardless of the adversary's repeated and rehearsed lies, they do not demolish God's truth. His truth reveals that you are predestined, foreseen, seen, called, appointed, and anointed. God is watching to see His Word fulfilled in your life.

It is time to believe, embrace, and live out the prophetic Word of God spoken over you before you were formed in your mother's womb (Jeremiah 1:5). It is time to connect the dots of your spiritual journey from pre-birth to birth to now. This is your preformation, and it has a destination with only your name on it!

Regardless of any concerns or inadequacies you may feel or experience, remember that not only did God set you apart while your mother was carrying you, but God set you apart from the beginning of time—pre-womb and even pre-time. Now that is amazing!

The Knowledge of God

The Message interprets Jeremiah 1:5 this way: "I knew all about you. Before you saw the light of day, I had holy plans for you: A prophet to the nations—that's what I had in mind for you." Beloved, God has holy plans that are uniquely designed just for you. Such plans were created and written in the heavens. Yahweh Elohim predestined a unique and divine plan for you in the celestial atmosphere, and nothing can destroy or separate you from His plan, and nothing can separate you from Him.

The apostle Paul says it best, "For I am convinced that neither death nor life, neither angels nor demons, neither the present nor the future, nor any powers, neither height nor depth, nor anything else in all creation, will be able to separate us from the love of God that is in Christ Jesus our Lord" (Romans 8:38–39). *No* thing and *no* one can separate you from God.

In Psalm 139, the psalmist "concentrates on one dimension of God's relation to human beings. 'You know me'—that is the theme of the whole plea, 'Know me so that you can lead me.'"[4] God knows you inside and out and is more than equipped and able to lead and guide you each and every step of the way.

You cannot be separated from God's infinite and intimate knowledge of and for you. His divine dimensions of knowledge about you existed before you were born and will continue to unfold throughout the journey of your life and into eternity.

As the Spirit uniquely unravels His plan for your life, He will unveil divine clarity. Your desire to know cannot be accelerated. Only in God's kairos time will He reveal His plans for you. There is no need to be anxious or worried. Just knowing that God's omnipotence, omniscience, and omnipresence are forever with you births a soul posture of confidential peace in Him. Shalom.

In his *Psalms* commentary, James Luther Mays expounds on this type of peace. He writes:

> The psalmist is free for and to God. God is the limit of his existence, yet he is himself a real person to God—accountable, confronted, known. God is free for and to the psalmist. The motions of God's relation to the psalmist transcends the psalmist's understanding. What he knows, he knows he does not know. His knowing is an unknowing: its achievement is wonder

> and the only certainty is "I am with you" (vv. 18, 6, 14).[5]

The psalmist is cognizant of the limitations of his personhood and his finite knowledge of himself. Likewise, you and I have limitations of ourselves. Nonetheless, it is incumbent upon us to prayerfully seek the mind and will of God (as much as humanly possible) with a humble desire to better understand His activity in our lives.[6]

Regardless of the knowledge we may obtain, the finiteness of our understanding and complete comprehension of ourselves will remain limited. As mere humans, we will always maintain a sense of unknowing. Yet, our security resides in the fact that God is all-knowing and that He is with us throughout the ups and downs of our limited lives.

Not only is He Immanuel, which means God with us, while we reside on earth, He is Immanuel throughout all time. He was with us in the past, He is with us in the present, and He will be with us throughout eternity.

I am continuously curious about the activity of God in the lives of people. He is present in the lives of people, whether they acknowledge Him or not. There is nowhere that anyone can go that He is not already there. The psalmist makes this very clear in Psalm 139. He was fully aware that wherever he went, God was already there. The psalmist says to Yahweh, "If I go up to the heavens, you are there; if I make my bed in the depths, you are there. If I rise on the wings of the dawn, if I settle on the far side of the sea, even there your hand will guide me, your right hand will hold me fast" (vv. 8–10). There was nowhere the psalmist could arrive where God was not already there.

Allow me to share a story with you to demonstrate that God is always with us and even before us. In 1996, God moved our family of three from Hillsborough, New

Jersey, to Charlotte, North Carolina. Once we settled into our new location, our daughter, Vérnee, started working at a local pizza restaurant. She drove my 1993 red Volvo to work. One day, while she was away at work, our good friend Gloria Potts stopped by to visit us, and she parked her red Volvo in our garage. When Vérnee came home and opened the garage door, she saw a red Volvo. She went into the house and shared the confusion she encountered upon arriving home. She told us that when she saw the red Volvo in the garage, she said to herself, "Am I already here?" We all found the red Volvo story hilarious. I would imagine that Vérnee felt a lot like the psalmist: she felt like what she was experiencing had already happened. In God's omnipresence, God arrives before us at every point in our lives. Unbeknownst to us, He is always before us and before we arrive. He is the *before*.

God Is Present in Our Journeys

One of my favorite pastimes is watching documentaries on television. I like to learn about people's lives and see the impact of their past on their present. From December 1, 2024, to January 5, 2025, my husband and I were on vacation in Hilton Head, South Carolina. During this time, I was blessed to enjoy documentaries on the lives of Barack Obama, Mother Teresa, Desi and Lucy, Michael Jackson, and Eddie Murphy. Other documentaries that I have watched over the years include stories on the lives of Elvis Presley, John F. Kennedy, Jackie Onassis, Martin Luther King Jr., Jimmy Carter, Michelle Obama, Tina Turner, Whitney Houston, Quincy Jones, Marilyn Monroe, Donald Trump, Lebron James, Kobe Bryant, Michael Jordan, Muhammad Ali, Malcolm X, Colin Kaepernick,

Colin Powell, Beyoncé, Alex Murdaugh, Lyle and Erik Menendez, Tiger Woods, Lady Diana, Harry & Meghan, Oprah Winfrey, Mary J. Blige, and more. Each story captured my attention as I sat on the edge of my seat, waiting to see how their past influenced their societal impact and how their lives unrolled. I enjoy watching documentaries, and a good book about a person also gets my full attention. The commonality of all these stories is the unveiling of their unique journeys.

Even though I had limited space while packing for our stay in Hilton Head, I felt the most impactful books I could bring during our stay would be books about the lives of spiritual leaders. Two of the books I brought were *Becoming Dallas Willard* by Gary W. Moon and Saint Augustine's *Confessions*.

The travel, research, and conversations that Gary Moon engaged in to write a biography of Dallas Willard are to be highly commended. In his book, Moon shares the multifaceted complexities of the philosophical spiritual giant, Dallas Willard. As Moon summarizes Willard's tumultuous childhood, he writes:

> In the midst of all the childhood pain, however, Dallas met a God he came to believe was the most joyous being in the universe, and nothing bad should ever be spoken or thought of him. Perhaps in part it was the contrast concerning his image of God and that of his father that made him realize God should not be created in the image of one's male parent, unless that parent bore a striking resemblance to the prodigal son's father. Perhaps the painful relationship with his own father motivated him to realize

> that we should never "let anyone tell you something bad about God."[7]

From this paragraph, it is evident that Dallas Willard's journey with God was not flawless. He had a turbulent childhood, but by the grace of God, Dr. Willard was propelled into ministry to fulfill God's purpose and plan for his life. God gave him wisdom to see the loving authenticity of the Godhead Father, in spite of the flaws of his earthly father. Experiencing God is His desire for all.

In the list of documentaries above, some of the featured people pressed through hard times to experience the presence of God in their lives, whereas others would never have such an encounter, whether in part or entirely. Whether one recognizes God's presence or not, He is always omnipresent. He knows what will happen before it happens.

Regardless of how the enemy may try to derail God's plan for one's life, God's hand will prevail. Attacks will come, and attacks will go, but God's plan will prevail. I do not believe that anyone who leaves this ole earth will be pain free. Dr. Willard's and the people's journeys in the stories were no exception.

We all have a before. We have a before that existed in the earth realm, and we have a time that points to the before that existed before this present moment. Today you are in the now, and yet an unknown future is forthcoming. Before you go dashing to what is yet unknown, take time to settle into the now.

There is no way to avoid the before, even before the very moment you are experiencing now, the previous moment was before. There is no way to get around the before. There is always a before. In multiple ways, your spiritual autobiography is consistently your before as you are on your way to the now, which leads to the after.

None of your life, whether before or now, will be perfect. Like Dallas Willard and the people in the documentaries, your life will not be without challenges. Willard had to honestly address the pain of his past and see God amidst the crises of his life. Therefore, as you begin this journey, make up your mind to face your truths even when it hurts. As I have watched numerous documentaries and read several autobiographies and biographies, I have seen how God's presence is constant in His creation. He does not leave His creation without His presence, nor does He shield His humanity from all the challenges of life. We do not live in a perfect, pain-free universe. Nor are we humans perfect.

We all have our inadequacies, similar to the imperfections of the prophet Jeremiah. There are no perfect human beings, and that includes you and me. Only One is perfect, and that is God. Humans are imperfect; thus, we must depend on Him to make it through the tight and inescapable traps and corners of life. Our imperfections call us to make a decision (or not) to completely depend on Him. He already knows our end from the beginning and consistently beckons us to draw nigh to Him for His divine help and support. If you and I desire to live a life dependent upon God, we cannot go through life without His presence. He makes the dots, and He connects the dots; He just desires that we see His activity throughout the course of our lifetime.

As we move forward in the book, at the end of each chapter, I encourage you to take "Selah Moments" before moving on to the next chapter. Be intentional about taking time to exhale. Pause. Reflect. Pray. Write. All the chapters end with Selah Moments that are uniquely designed to better prepare you to write your personal spiritual autobiography.

You may notice that each Selah Moment ends with the

suffix "-ING," which signifies action. In my book *Spiritual Practices for Soul Care: 40 Ways to Deepen Your Faith*, all the practices also conclude with "-ING." This was not accidental—it was a deliberate and meaningful choice. The "-ING" not only represents ongoing spiritual activity, but it also serves as an acronym: I Need God. To fully engage in these Selah Moments you and I must recognize our dependence on God. Indeed, we need Him—continually and completely. It is now that we begin!

SELAH MOMENTS

PAUSING—Take a few deep breaths as you pause and think about what you have learned in chapter 1.

REFLECTING—Give yourself ample time to reflect on your preformation. Reflect on how God is speaking directly to your soul, based on your reading of this chapter. What do you sense God saying to you?

PRAYING—Pray about how this chapter may apply specifically to your spiritual journey. Please google "The Creation" by James Weldon Johnson. I encourage you to read this poem twice. Thank God for His creation as you read. Thank Him for creating humanity. Thank Yahweh Elohim for preforming, forming, and creating you.

WRITING—Even though in this chapter there is no need to write, it is a good time to spiritually, mentally, and emotionally prepare your heart and mind to write your spiritual autobiography. Consider writing questions or thoughts about your beginning that you would like to explore.

Chapter 2

DEAR DIARY

Then the Lord *replied: "Write down the revelation and make it plain on tablets so that a herald may run with it."*
Habakkuk 2:2

While growing up as a young teenager, my diary became my best friend. She was always there when I needed to share my thoughts. She was there during times of laughter and times of sorrow. She was there when I burst into puberty with questions galore. She was there when I shared my doubts and fears. She never judged me, and I always knew I could trust her with my innermost thoughts. Daily, I would go to her and share how I felt. With her, I could confide the depth of my soul and share memories I dared not share with anyone else. She was a safe space. I could share extended stories, or I could briefly share an immediate thought with her. It just depended on the moment and my mood. Whether I wrote in pencil or ink, it did not matter, because my communication with my diary was private, and I knew what I wrote within the lines of her pages would not be shared with anyone.

My level of confidence with her was extremely high. In particular, I felt secure with our sharing because she had a key that only I knew where it was kept. Even if someone wanted to pry into her, they could not because she was locked, safe, and secure. The diary was leather-bound and had cream pages. Within her three-by-five walls, everything was top secret.

I could not wait to tell her about my first kiss. In my mind, it was tremendously gross, and I could not wait to get home and wash my mouth out with peroxide. Thinking of all the germs exchanged during kissing was enough for me to freak out. In my diary, I could share the complexities and uncertainties of my innermost soul without any repercussions of judgment. I could go to her and express silly thoughts about who I liked and who I thought liked me. As a teenager, many moments felt overwhelming—like having pimples, being the right age to wear stockings and heels, going to the prom, while watching my body change and be framed in front of my eyes. As a studious learner, it was important to me to examine daily classroom topics, the teacher's input, and the various perspectives and interpretations of my classmates that often differed, even though we shared the same learning settings.

Dear Diary, thank you for always being my sole confidant. Little did I know you were foundational for my passion for writing, as well as a tool to express my innermost thoughts. My memories of you are marvelous, and spending time with you allowed me to wrestle with the vicissitudes of my life early on. I may not call you Diary anymore. Now, I define you as journaling, or reflecting, or even perhaps my first stab at writing an autobiography. Even though our teenage years together were spiritual, I do not recall having a tremendous amount of spiritual things on my mind during those formative adolescent years.

As I matured, I grew from writing on the lined pages of my three-by-five soft-covered diary to writing on three-ring lined notebook paper. Over the years, I finally purchased and began to write in a real journal. Here I am decades later, and I still find joy in jotting down my secretive thoughts and writing about life occurrences. Over the years, I have written about multiple benchmarks in my life. Below is a brief draft of a few experiences on my soul journey. This is an example of an outline that can be used as a preparatory tool for writing your story. However, the guideline in chapter 8 is more comprehensive.

Please note, it is not necessary for you to have a diary; the main point is for you to prayerfully seek to recall the earlier years of your journey. We all remember pivotal points that occurred in different areas. There is no right or wrong to the process. The objective is to seek to recall and reflect.

AGES ONE TO TWENTY
YOUR FIRST QUARTER OF LIFE

Dear Diary: One to Ten Years of Age

- Born the fourth of five children (Mama really wanted a boy as she already had three girls).
- On February 22, 1954, I was born in Columbus County Hospital.
- I was named Barbara Jeanette Lewis.
- I grew up on a farm.
- Some called me "Bob" for short.
- I enjoyed playing with my dolls, reading, and sewing.
- I attended Mount Olive High School.
- Our great-grandfather was one of the founders of the school.
- I loved my friends, teachers, and learning.
- I left home and moved to Baltimore, Maryland.

- I lived in a community in Baltimore called Cherry Hill.
- I lived with Aunt Melba (my mother's sister) and Uncle John.
- I attended Carter G. Woodson Elementary School.
- My favorite grade teachers were Mr. Petza and Mrs. Smith.

Dear Diary: Eleven to Twenty Years of Age

- I moved from Baltimore, Maryland, back to North Carolina.
- I had lots of why questions when I had to be uprooted again.
- I moved back to the farm in Whiteville, North Carolina.
- The adjustment was challenging.
- I felt isolated.
- I gave my life to the Lord.
- At the age of fourteen, God moved in my heart during the fall revival of 1967.

  I was so excited when I made my way down to the mourner's bench.

  I accepted Jesus Christ while the ladies told me how much Jesus loved me.

  I was thrilled!
- This was the beginning of an amazing journey with Jesus.
- In 1969, the schools were integrated.
- We were bused to school.
- In 1972, I graduated from West Columbus High School in Cerro Gordo, North Carolina.

- I graduated with honors.
  - I was a member of the Beta Club.
  - I was a member of the National Honor Society.
  - I was a finalist in the "Make It Yourself Wool Contest" (sewing and design contest).
- In the fall of 1972, I attended North Carolina Central University in Durham, North Carolina.
  - I majored in clothing and textiles, and fashion and design.
  - I was a member of Who's Who Among American Universities and Colleges.
  - I experienced my first love, but got heartbroken.
  - I pledged Delta Theta Sigma Sorority.
  - I graduated early and with honors!

Spring 1975—Line of Delta Sigma Theta at North Carolina Central University. Outfits designed and sewn by Barbara Lewis and Bebra Guin. Used by permission.

AGES TWENTY-ONE TO FORTY YOUR SECOND QUARTER OF LIFE

Dear Diary: Twenty-One to Thirty Years of Age

- In 1976, I began working for Maas Brothers Department Store in Tampa, Florida.

I was the manager of the junior department.

I met my husband, Gilbert L. Peacock.

I really fell in love!

- In 1978, I moved to Denver, Colorado.

  We had a small wedding at Union Baptist Church in Denver, Colorado.

  I gave birth to our one and only daughter, Vérnee Ivy Peacock (Note the initials, V.I.P.).

  I worked at Allstate Insurance Company.

- We moved to Uniondale, New York.

  We bought our first home.

  It was a lovely red brick Cape Cod.

- I began working, even though I had a baby.

  I went door to door selling Avon Cosmetics.

  This provided some funds.

  It was a joy to meet many people in the community.

  I was blessed to work in the garment industry (the rag business).

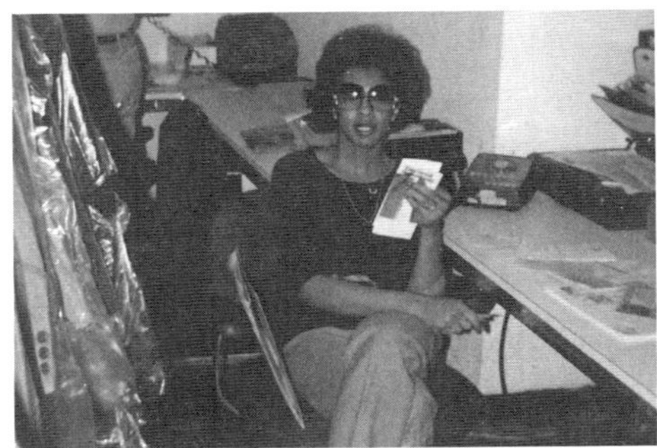

Photo from author's collection; used with permission.

What a blessing to work on 7th Avenue in New York City!

My first job in Manhattan was with Mondi of America, a German company.

My second job in Manhattan was with Harvé Bernard, a Jewish company.

It was a pleasure to attend classes at the Fashion Institute of Technology (FIT) in New York City.

- We moved to Hamden, Connecticut.

  We met lifelong friends.

  My mentor was Apostle Bernice Gibbs (husband Reggie).

  I met my best friend, Rhonda Jones (husband Kenneth "Ken").

  I was hired to work in sales and to assist with buying at a local department store.

Dear Diary: Thirty-One to Forty Years of Age

This was a major learning phase.

- Life was all about learning how to be a young wife to a husband who worked in corporate America.

  My husband's career took us around the country.

  We lived in six states and purchased eleven homes.

  In some states, we purchased more than one home in a particular town.

  Three of the homes we built from the ground up.

- During this age range, life was about learning the importance of being the best adult I could be.

  Life demanded I discern my values and priorities.

  This required seeking God to help me balance home and work.

- During this age range, I became passionate about studying the Word of God.

  Daily I would read about the virtuous woman in Proverbs 31.

  One of my other favorite books was *Becoming a Woman of Excellence* by Cynthia Heald.
- In 1983, we moved to Hillsborough, New Jersey.

  I attended Bible Study Fellowship.

  I worked at Erika's Boutique.

  I opened Bavar's Fashion Boutique (the dream of my life).

AGES FORTY-ONE TO SIXTY
YOUR THIRD QUARTER OF LIFE

Dear Diary: Forty-One to Fifty Years of Age

- We moved to Rochester Hills, Michigan, in 1992.

  This was a hard move (to a colder climate).

  This was a God move, even though I did not fully understand it.

  In June 1992, I was licensed to preach at Newman AME Church.

  This church is located in Pontiac, Michigan.

  The senior pastor was Pastor Donald George Harwell.

  During our tenure, I taught at a community Bible study.
- We moved to Hillsborough, New Jersey, in 1994.

  We attended First Baptist Church of Lincoln Gardens (Pastor Charlie Brown).

I graduated from Princeton Theological Seminary in 1994.

- We moved to Charlotte, North Carolina, in 1996.

  My first job out of seminary was working at Mount Carmel Baptist Church.

  This was my first ministry job.

  It was a joy to serve alongside Pastor Dr. Casey Kimbrough.

- I taught at Queen City Bible College.

  This was a delight.

  Working with the students was so rewarding.

  The pastor was Bishop Phillip Davis.

- After Mount Carmel, I began working at University Park Baptist Church in 1999.

  Rev. Claude Richard Alexander Jr. was the Senior Pastor.

  In 2001, the new name for the church became The Park Church.

  It is a megachurch.

  During my tenure, I served as Minister of Discipleship and Prayer.

  While working here, I wrote my first book with a team.

  The book is entitled *Called to Teach*. The acronym CALLED stands for Commissioned As Leaders, Learners, Educators, and Disciples.

  Thank you, Urban Ministries, for your support in publishing the book.

I am so thankful to have this photo of my first book with Bishop Claude Richard Alexander Jr. This picture was taken at the Hampton Ministers Conference, Urban Ministries Bookstore on the campus of Hampton University, Hampton, Virginia. Photo from author's collection; used with permission

Dear Diary: Fifty-One to Sixty Years of Age

- I never saw surgery in my future.

  I had knee surgery.

  As an intercessor and prayer warrior, explaining sickness can make you feel very vulnerable.

  But no matter what, God still heals, and He heals however and whenever He desires.
- In 2005, I had a nervous breakdown.
- During this season of life, I was experiencing:

  perimenopause

  anxiety

  burnout

  depression
- The wall of life came tumbling down, and I totally shut down!
- In 2005, our daughter Vérnee married our lovely son-in-love, Mr. Michael Wilkinson (November 5, 2005).

- Our first grandchild was born.

  Her name is Eden.

  She was born on February 17, 2007, in Fort Walton Beach, Florida.
- For my doctoral degree, I attended Gordon-Conwell Theological Seminary (South Hamilton, Massachusetts) from 2009 to 2013.

  I received my doctorate in Spiritual Formation for Ministry Leaders.

  The professors for the cohort were Dr. David Currie and Dr. Stephen Macchia.
- God called me to resign from my position at the Park Church in July 2013.

  God emphatically called me out of full-time ministry.

  I knew if I did not obey, my future would not exist.

  God showed me my future, and if I were disobedient, it would not be pretty.

AGES SIXTY-ONE TO EIGHTY
YOUR FOURTH QUARTER OF LIFE

Dear Diary: Sixty-One to Seventy Years of Age

- Barbara L. Peacock Ministries was founded in December 2013.

  We are committed to "providing safe spaces for encounters with God."

  We do this through gatherings that provide praying, teaching, and retreating.

  Thank you, Billy Graham Evangelistic Association, for providing us with our initial space.

- I had heart surgery in January 2014.

  This had to be the most devastating part of my life.

  I was born with a mitral valve prolapse.

  The heart surgery almost took me out, but thanks be to God, I am still here!

  After surgery, my husband informed me that another lady had died from surgery.

  It is by the grace of God that I endured and healed over several months.

- I wrote and self-published a journal entitled *Psalm 119 Scriptural Journal*.

  This was my second book.

  Even though it is pretty simple, it took me years to write and format it.

- God used me to write an award-winning book.

  The title is *Soul Care in African American Practice*.

  It was published by InterVarsity Press.

  Soul Care in African American Practice has a complimentary workbook.

  Thank you Urban Ministries for the support with the workbook.

  I am committing the remainder of my years to writing.

- I founded Peacock Soul Care.

  This institute offers certificates in Spiritual Direction and Spiritual Formation.

  We are the first African American Institute to offer such certificates.

  We also offer enrichment classes and a leadership track.

- Onto the back of our home, I built a porch for ministry, retreats, and writing.

  This project should have taken only three months.

  The work on this project spanned more than a year.

  The most frustrating adventure yet, but God!
- My second sabbatical was at seventy.

  I cut my natural hair really short.

  This was a freedom move.

  I love it!
- I wrote the book entitled *Soul Journey: Transform Your Present by Rediscovering God in Your Past.*

Dear Diary's Story

And, as you know, the list goes on, and on, and on. These are just a few benchmarks that occurred between elementary school and now. Yes, while my diary writing led to journaling, I did not know the benefits of what some would consider a menial task. This simple and innocent discipline led to the practice of reflecting and writing. Now, I have expanded my diary skills, and I am writing books. Thank You, Jesus!

I had no idea how writing in my diary would be a foundational and impacting tool that God would use to catapult me into encouraging others to write their spiritual autobiographies. From writing in my diary, I learned the importance of all of us telling our stories and the benefits we all experience when we get our thoughts out of the walls of our minds and onto paper (or a computer).

Allow me to write out what some of the above bullet points may look like in an actual document to guide you in writing and reflecting on your own journey. Here goes part of my story:

On July 5th, 1978, Gilbert L. Peacock and I said, "I do" at Union Baptist Church in Denver, Colorado. Pastor Bowen officiated our very small wedding. Herman and Alice Peacock, Permella Lewis, Linda Rivere, and Curtis Lennon were our guests. Now, that is small!

I am thankful we did not enter into holy matrimony without a three-strand cord (Ecclesiastes 4:12). Spirit God was in our midst and has graciously kept my husband and me together for forty-seven years. In a place over a thousand miles away from our birth homes, respectively, Whiteville, North Carolina (Barbara), and Tallahassee, Florida (Gilbert), God abided among us. To this humble union, God birthed an amazing baby girl. We named her Vérnee Ivy Peacock (V.I.P.). During the first half of our marriage, Gilbert worked in sales in the chemical industry. His job in corporate America required us to relocate often. Sometimes we would stay in a city for less than a year. We were always on the move. Our relocations include:

- Denver, Colorado
- Uniondale, New York (Long Island)
- Hamden, Connecticut
- Neshanic Station, New Jersey
- Rochester Hills, Michigan
- Colleyville, Texas
- Hillsborough, New Jersey
- Charlotte, North Carolina
- Waxhaw, North Carolina
- Uptown, Charlotte, North Carolina
- Huntersville, North Carolina

- Waxhaw, North Carolina
- Indian Trail, North Carolina

In 1978, we lived in Denver. While we were in Denver, I worked for Allstate Insurance Company. In 1979, Diamond Shamrock Corporation transferred our family to Long Island, New York. Vérnee was just a few months old when we dedicated her to Christ in Bethel AME Church, Freeport (Long Island). Her godmother (my college roommate), Bebra Guin (now Evans), was kind enough to join us in the dedication. I remember being a young mother and sharing my insecurities with my mother, Sarah Peacock Lewis. I can hear her say, "Babies need lots of love and lots of attention." This was the best advice anyone could have given me, and I still try to abide by that mantra today.

While we lived in Uniondale, Long Island, I began my postcollege career. The first thing I did was sell Avon Products door to door. Then I was able to get a job as a cashier at Marshalls. I knew neither of these was a long-term job; however, it was good to do something and get out of the house. In addition, I was blessed to work in New York City at Mondi of America (1411 Broadway) and Harvé Bernard (205 West 39th Street). Every day, I was so excited to go to work in the "Rag Business." There was nothing more thrilling than walking on 7th Avenue in my three-inch heels and the latest fashion. I would take the train from Hempstead to Penn Station and then walk to my job location.

In 1980, God moved us to New Jersey. Here we enjoyed being members of First Baptist Church of Lincoln Gardens (in Somerset, New Jersey) under the leadership first of Dr. Charlie H. Brown Jr., who preceded Dr. Deforest "Buster" Soaries Jr. While living in New Jersey, Gilbert began to work for Linden Chemicals and Plastic (LCP

Chemicals). Their corporate headquarters was in Edison, New Jersey. During our tenure in New Jersey, my business partner, Barbara Gianettino, and I opened up Bavar's Fashion Boutique. This was truly a dream come true for both Barbara and me. God bless Barbara. She was truly my best friend. She passed in her Warren, New Jersey, home in 2022, and I was asked by her family (Mr. Gianettino, Vicky, and Ronnie) to offer her eulogy. Needless to say, I was honored to serve.

In 1992, God saw fit to move our family to Rochester Hills, Michigan. At Newman African Methodist Episcopal (AME) Church, in Pontiac, Michigan, I preached (maybe taught . . . only God knows which) my initial sermon. This had to be the most humbling experience in my whole life. A year later, we were transferred and found a beautiful home in Colleyville, Texas. Who would have ever thought that such a life could exist? For sure, not me. Yes, before I was born, God knew (Psalm 139).

In the summer of 1993, my husband's German-based company, Hoechst Celanese, transferred us from Rochester Hills, Michigan, to Dallas–Fort Worth, Texas. As corporate transferees, once again, we were in search of a church home, a physical home, a school, doctors, grocery stores, and so much more. It was just the three of us (our daughter, Vérnee, my husband, Gilbert, and me). Our concerns included finding a Spirit-filled Bible teaching church, a good school, and a home that was located in a safe and upwardly mobile community.

We were looking for homes in an area that we discerned best suited our lifestyle preferences. We were in prayer that God would lead us to the right school where our daughter would receive the best education. Back in those days, we chose the school system based on the SAT scores for the prospective school. And the town of Colleyville and the

Grapevine area had good scores for junior high school. In these prospective areas were beautiful homes, and one in particular caught my eye. When I first saw it, it was way out of our price range, but I could not erase it from my mind.

We kept looking and looking and looking for the home of our dreams. We even made an offer on a house, but it did not come through. Then I felt directed by the Spirit to ask my husband if we could take another look at a home that had previously caught my eye. I must admit, not only did it capture my physical eye, but it also captured my heart. And to our surprise, when we went back, the price had dropped $50,000. I was like, "Oh my, how could this be?" It must have been God. This was next to impossible. But "remember, Barbara, with God, all things are possible." Even though my husband had some doubts, we made an offer to the builder. I remember like yesterday, us pulling up to the phone booth in a Kmart shopping center in Colleyville. He left me in the car and went to the phone booth to call the builder. To our dismay, the builder did not accept the offer. So, we continued to discuss alternative plans for our new home; however, my faith remained strong.

That night, we returned to the hotel room and had a good night's sleep. Upon rising the next day, my husband decided to meet with the builder once again. While he was negotiating with the builder, I was in the hotel room praying prayers of faith. I reminded God of His promise that He revealed to me when we were viewing the home. During this time, I sensed God saying, "If I bless you with this home, will you pray as far as you can see as you stand facing the horizon?"

The house sat on a hill, with a clear peripheral view of downtown Dallas. From the room on the third floor,

I could see the tall buildings in the city, and I could see the airplanes in the air as they took off and landed. I said "yes" to God. My covenant with God was to pray over the Dallas area and the surrounding cities of Fort Worth, Grapevine, and Colleyville. I said, "Yes." So, when the builder told my husband "no," I was confused. In my spirit, I knew that I really needed to press into the heart of God. As I lay in that hotel room, I was reminded of God's promise. Upon rehearsing my conversation with the Lord in my mind, I pulled the hotel covers over my head and proceeded to put God in remembrance of His promise. I was a young lady desperate to see God move, and I believed that He would.

The lesson to be learned here is that no matter how many no's you may receive, if God has a yes, no doubt or fear can hinder His promises. When God makes you a promise and it looks like it is not going to come to fruition, that is the time that God is calling you to press in spiritually and to put Him in remembrance of His Word. If He said He would do it, He will do it, and no demon in hell can stop His promises or His plans. That is exactly how faith works. Therefore, relax, reignite your faith, and watch faith work. Watch God do exactly what He said He would do. Assuredly, faith without works is definitely dead (James 2:17). Show God your faith in action, and watch Him respond to your persistence. This is a "But God" moment. Like me, there will come a time in your life that you may have to pull some covers over your head and cry out, "God, you said!" I believe that once you put God in remembrance of His promise(s), God will respond to His Word. And when He does, you will see the manifestation of God following through.

Faith roots and a proven track record with Yahweh are great assets to have on your spiritual journey. I am very appreciative that early on in my life, God allowed me to be surrounded by a family that was grounded with faith-based roots.

I grew up in very humble beginnings in rural North Carolina, in a little town called Whiteville. Growing up on the farmland of Whiteville was one of the greatest blessings of my life. Even though we were what some would consider poor, I did not know we were poor. As far as I was concerned, our lifestyle and financial status were normal, and everybody around us was normal. Regardless of what we did not have, we always had faith, and we always had God, and that is enough.

We were a family who went to church on Sundays. Part of our legacy was that we were a family who loved to sing, and many members of our family were musically inclined. My late sister, Permella Wyvonnie Lewis, was the choir director of two local churches. We could go to "the Baptist church," Mount Olive Missionary Baptist, on the first and third Sundays. We attended "the holiness church," Floyd Temple #2, on the second and fourth Sundays. Back in the day, church choirs would proudly march into the sanctuary while singing at the beginning of the worship service. One song, in particular, that comes to mind and is ruminating in my soul is entitled "We've Come This Far by Faith," composed by Albert A. Goodson in 1963. The lyrics remind us of how far faith has carried us as we leaned on God.

There are numerous renditions of this song. One of my favorites is a beautiful rendition sung by Pastor Donnie McClurkin. It can be found on YouTube.[1] I believe that this song will be a tremendous blessing to you when you listen to it.

I pray that the spiritual journey bullets and written story I shared above will be instrumental in writing your story. Even though I have written a short version in the past, every time I write part of my story I see more and more of God's activity in my life. Moreover, this time, I am publicly declaring that I intend to write my memoir. Glory be to God! The bullets provide an illustration that can also be the beginning of writing my more in-depth spiritual autobiography. I will probably name it around the theme "Peacock." In your writing, the purpose of writing out bullets is for you to be able to connect the dots of your journey, like I have.

You may or may not have written in a diary. It does not matter. What matters is where you are today as you follow God's lead with a desire for Him to make you a better disciple in the kingdom. So here we are. Let's go. Let's buckle in for this transformative journey. I promise you will be glad you did.

SELAH MOMENTS

PAUSING—Take a few deep breaths as you pause and think about what you have learned in this chapter. What were the points about my story that connected with your story?

REFLECTING—Reflect on your intake and how God speaks directly to you. Based on your reading of Dear Diary, what do you sense God saying to you?

PRAYING—Pray about how my story may apply specifically to your spiritual journey. How is your life different from mine?

WRITING—Even now, you are spiritually, mentally, and emotionally preparing to write your spiritual autobiography. Do not hesitate to jot down anything that may be stirring in your heart that you do not want to forget.

Chapter 3

A SPIRITUAL AUTOBIOGRAPHY

Jesus did many other things as well. If every one of them were written down, I suppose that even the whole world would not have room for the books that would be written.

John 21:25

I used the term *spiritual autobiography* several times in the previous chapter. Let us now take a close look at the terminology around this topic. This language of spiritual autobiography may be new to some, and for others, you may be very familiar with the subject matter. But before I dive into an extended definition of a spiritual autobiography, let me break the meaning down to its simplest form to ensure we're working from the same definition.

The phrase *spiritual autobiography* has various components, and breaking each word apart will be beneficial.

- Spiritual
    Spirit (as in the Holy Spirit)
    spirit (as in *your* spirit)

- Autobiography
  auto
  biography

The mere word *spiritual* sets the tone that writing our spiritual autobiography is a spiritual event. The root word in spiritual is Spirit. The writing of your story is from the Holy Spirit to your spirit. Your story is guided by God's Spirit (the Holy Spirit) and is revealed to your human spirit. "Spiritual" connotes the involvement of all the components of God's Spirit and the human spirit working together with one goal. Spiritual involves the activity of the Holy Spirit and the human spirit working together for an appointed or identified result. In this context, the word *spiritual* is an adjective that modifies the kind of autobiography that is to be written.

Auto refers to self. It is all about the story of your soul. Yes, it can be authentically and centrally all about you for once! So, go ahead and plop yourself down in the middle of the story and allow all your truths to emerge with no hindrance, condemnation, or falsification. In this book, you will learn about writing *your* spiritual autobiography; no one can do it for you but you! No substitutes.

The word *biography* refers to the story or history of your life. That is exciting! The objective of this book is to teach you about writing your spiritual autobiography and to guide you along a process designed to empower you to reflect on your past, take a good long look into your spiritual mirrors, and see how the activity and hand of God have worked in your life and are working in your life. It is your story, for His glory! Really, His story.

Defining a Spiritual Autobiography

A spiritual autobiography is a nonfiction story about significant events, people, and places that have influenced your relationship with God. It is designed for you to write about the spiritual benchmarks in your life where you have encountered God's hand moving. Such writing includes peaks, valleys, faith-filled moments, and doubt-filled moments.

A spiritual autobiography denotes your faith development process. This process is done intentionally while listening to what God is saying. Honesty is essential. Be willing to look at your journey's good and difficult parts.

Simply put, a spiritual autobiography is an introspective perspective of yourself that provides a written document from as far back as you can remember into the present. This written document is your personal explorative and transformative narrative. During the writing of this self-reflective experience, prayerfully anticipate God's healing power to emerge as He imparts wisdom, knowledge, and understanding into your very soul.

Writing your spiritual autobiography will help you better understand the complexities and challenges of your journey. When ministering to leaders, counseling other believers, or providing soul care and spiritual direction, I highly recommend that the people I am working with write their spiritual autobiographies. This is a tool that I have personally found very helpful during my sessions in spiritual direction and soul care. During these sessions, the spiritual autobiography is a great entry point for our initial discussion. In addition, when shared in a group format, the spiritual autobiography provides a source for people to see the connectivity and correlation of God's activity around them.

Tragedies such as losing parents, divorce, and feelings of abandonment may cause you to ask God, "Where were You?" In the midst of difficult questions, it is good to remind yourself that God was there—and still is.

A scriptural text that supports the discipline of writing

your spiritual autobiography is Psalm 139. The psalmist writes:

> For You formed my inward parts;
> You covered me in my mother's womb.
> I will praise You, for I am fearfully and
> wonderfully made;
> Marvelous are Your works,
> And that my soul knows very well.
> My frame was not hidden from You,
> When I was made in secret,
> And skillfully wrought in the lowest parts
> of the earth.
> Your eyes saw my substance, being yet
> unformed.
> And in Your book they all were written,
> The days fashioned for me,
> When as yet there were none of them.
>
> How precious also are Your thoughts to me,
> O God!
> How great is the sum of them!
> If I should count them, they would be more
> in number than the sand;
> When I awake, I am still with You.
> (vv. 13–18 NKJV)

Eugene Peterson imagines the passage this way:

> Oh yes, you shaped me first inside, then
> out;
> you formed me in my mother's womb.
> I thank you, High God—you're
> breathtaking!

Body and soul, I am marvelously made!
I worship in adoration—what a creation!
You know me inside and out,
you know every bone in my body;
You know exactly how I was made, bit by
bit,
how I was sculpted from nothing into
something.
Like an open book, you watched me grow
from conception to birth;
all the stages of my life were spread out
before you,
The days of my life all prepared
before I'd even lived one day.

Your thoughts—how rare, how beautiful!
God, I'll never comprehend them!
I couldn't even begin to count them—
any more than I could count the sand of
the sea.
Oh, let me rise in the morning and live always
with you!

In both readings, it is clear that the psalmist is writing his spiritual autobiography. We see how God's Spirit interacts from the beginning with the human spirit. God uniquely created each human. Before conception, God designed a purpose and a plan for everyone. From conception to birth and from birth until now, God has orchestrated unique journeys for every individual. Each soul is marvelously made to worship Yahweh Elohim and honor His sovereignty in their life.

The benefits of writing your life story are enormous. Have you ever wondered how the pieces of your life all fit together? Have you ever asked why God allowed specific incidents to happen or not to happen? Have you asked yourself, "Why do bad things happen to good people?" If you have asked any of these questions, writing your story will better equip you to answer some of your most probing questions. The nuances of life never cease to amaze me, and the questions that parallel them continue to unveil themselves if we look for them.

With a Bachelor of Arts in Fashion and Design from North Carolina Central University, a Master of Arts in Christian Education from Princeton Theological Seminary, and a Doctorate of Ministry in Spiritual Formation for Ministry Leaders from Gordon-Conwell Theological Seminary, I have dedicated decades of my life to seeking to better understand God's hand and activity in my life and the lives of others. Because of my passion for helping others find clarity in the journey, I pray that this book clears the way for you to see God's purpose in your life.

Contemplation and a Spiritual Autobiography

I grew up on a farm in the sandy land of southeastern North Carolina. The 125 acres that my great-granddaddy, Walter Peacock, purchased in the early twentieth century resided between Bladen and Columbus Counties. Currently, 25 acres remain in our family.

We had peach, pecan, apple, and walnut trees on our family farm. We grew tomatoes, cucumbers, greens, cabbage, okra, potatoes, peanuts, etc. The big crop that provided income was tobacco. Our farm animals included cows, pigs, chickens, horses, dogs, and cats. As a child, I loved to read, sew, and write. The setting of the acreage, the farm life, and my habits were instrumental in my contemplative development.

I was the child who always asked, "Why?" Sometimes,

asking a lot of questions got on my mother's nerves. She called me Henry Ellis because we had a neighbor with that name, and he was notorious for asking questions. This quest to know is why you are preparing to write your spiritual autobiography. Just wanting to be in the know is a good enough reason.

As a contemplative child and now a contemplative adult, I am mindful of the calm richness of the farmland and the spiritual legacy that came with it. My spiritual roots are deep in the land of the South. I love the smell of rain on the sandy dirt road. I love the rainy time of year, which is the season for gathering farm crops. I like to see things grow and get even more excited when the crops begin to flourish in their unique season and timing. There is nothing better than witnessing the activity of God during such moments. How beautifully Henri Nouwen expounds on the reflective life. He writes:

> Contemplative life is a human response to the fundamental fact that the central things in life, although spiritually perceptible, remain invisible in large measure and can very easily be overlooked by the inattentive, busy, distracted person that each of us can so readily become. The contemplative looks not so much around things but through them into their center. Through their center he discovers the world of spiritual beauty that is more real, has more matter. In effect, the beauty of physical matter is a reflection of its inner content.[1]

I am most humbled when I reflect on how the Lord allowed me to be born in a space providing such a spiritually beautiful setting. I immensely appreciate all my farmland roots and how God used them to prepare me with a heart that seeks to spiritually grasp the activity and power of His handiwork in and on the life of a soul. I am thankful for my parents and ancestors who valued the soil of the soul and had the stick-with-it persistence to nurture the farm even when the land was dry, and the soil was hard to cultivate. Their tedious tenacity, farmland hands, and cultivating spirits taught me to toil the soil as I seek to unravel the curious questions of the soul. Simply put, through the entire activity of writing your spiritual autobiography, I'm asking you to toil the soil of your soul.

Throughout this book, you will mentally look into a mirror that faces your soul as you seek to peek into the crevices of God's activity in and through you. You will mentally look back as far as you can remember until the present. Such seeking is designed to provide better discernment of your spiritual journey. You will reflect on the hand of God during your daily encounters with God, yourself, and others. As you commit to exploring your spiritual journey, you will prayerfully receive a better understanding of yourself and God's activity in your life. Consequently, soul transformation will occur.

Tending your soul through writing your spiritual autobiography will cause you to value who you were before you were formed in your mother's womb and who you are today. When you reflect on your spiritual journey, you care for your soul. Such an activity requires welcoming and honoring God into every phase of your life.

Writing your spiritual autobiography provides a contemplative and reflective foundation essential for living your best life. The central portion of writing your spiritual autobiography occurs during your initial writing. However, updating your autobiography is a lifelong process. Your earthly story never ends until you take your last breath, and your life beyond is unknown to your earthly soul. Writing your spiritual autobiography is one of the best gifts you can give yourself. I pray that as a result of engaging in this discipline, you will more effectively connect the dots of your life with God and others. I pray that the Spirit will reveal revelation, knowledge, wisdom, and impart understanding that you did not have before this assignment.

The writer of Proverbs tells us, "The beginning of wisdom is this: Get wisdom. Though it cost all you have, get understanding. Cherish her, and she will exalt you; embrace her, and she will honor you. She will give you a garland to grace your head and present you with a glorious crown" (Proverbs 4:7–9). The writing of your spiritual autobiography births understanding and imparts wisdom into your soul that you would not have otherwise experienced. It is truly God's grace that has kept you throughout the journey.

I am most appreciative that God firmly nudged me to write this book. I believe this is a game changer for the faith community. As Maya Angelou said, "If you don't know where you've come from, you don't know where you're going."[2] Understanding and taking the time to contemplate your journey brings clarity to your journey and opens you up to be more receptive to another person's journey.

Too often, we judge others without seeking to comprehend their motives for doing what they do. Once you have a firmer grasp on understanding your journey, you are more likely to be open to embracing another person's journey. However, when one is preoccupied with one's own stuff, there is little to no room to understand another's life story.

SELAH MOMENTS

PAUSING—Take a few deep breaths as you pause and consider what you learned in this chapter.

REFLECTING—Reflect on your intake, how God is speaking directly to you, and the call to take time for a deeper contemplation of your journey.

PRAYING—Pray about you. Yes, you! It is revolutionizing not to feel guilty when you think about yourself. Thinking about yourself is not selfish. Clothe your thinking with thanksgiving for how Yahweh Elohim, God our Creator, has intentionally carved out a space in heaven and on earth with you in mind.

WRITING—Even now, you are spiritually, mentally, and emotionally preparing to write your spiritual autobiography as you reflect on God's work and plan in you!

Chapter 4

BIBLICAL FOUNDATION FOR A SPIRITUAL AUTOBIOGRAPHY

In the beginning was the Word, and the Word was with God, and the Word was God.
John 1:1

From the first book of the Bible, Genesis, to the last book, Revelation, we find numerous biblical stores about thousands of characters. There are stories about people with names and some without names. Sometimes the stories are told about someone else. But both Testaments also provide biblical anecdotes of characters writing their spiritual autobiography, which isn't surprising. God is known for His desire to have a relationship with humanity, and one of the purposes of writing our stories is to reveal evidence of God's presence. Conclusively, both the Old and the New Testaments exemplify paradigms of God's desire for His human creation to have a relationship with Him.

Old Testament Journey

Creating humanity in God's image was God's original plan from the inception of time. With God's divine mindset, God saw fit to make His beloved humanity in His image. In Chapter 1, I shared the creation story found in Genesis 1:26–28.[1] Within this passage, the revelation of the inception of humanity is defined.

Throughout the canon, a variety of stories are written about the life, journey, and personal encounters of numerous biblical characters. In the book of Genesis, we find the first parents of creation, Adam and Eve. The crux of their story and their relationship with Yahweh is found in the first four chapters of Genesis. In Genesis 4:1, Adam expresses intimate love to his wife, Eve. She becomes pregnant and gives birth to their son Cain. She said, "With the help of the LORD I have brought forth a man." Afterward, the genealogy of the union of Adam and Eve and the first family continues. In Genesis 7, most of creation is wiped out during the flood. However, God chose to procreate the world through the seed of Noah and his family.

Genesis 12 shares the story of Abram and Sarai, whose names change to Abraham and Sarah after they become the parents of Isaac. Later we read that Isaac's wife, Rebecca, gave birth to Jacob, whose name was changed to Israel. He was the father of twelve sons, from whom were born the twelve tribes of Israel (God's chosen people).

The book of Genesis calls God's people to understand their identity anew. We are creatures of the one Creator God.[2] Not only is the book of Genesis pertinent to understanding our identity, but it is also a great resource filled with stories depicting the genealogy of God's first families. God's relationship with His chosen people continues with judges, kings, queens, and prophets. These stories shine tremendous light on leaders and are designed to help us better understand our identity and the like-minded thinking and behavior of humanity.

The Old Testament provides us with a plethora of stories. Likewise, we find amazing stories in the New Testament. Two of the most prominent figures in the New Testament are Jesus and the apostle Paul.

Jesus's Journey

Found in the gospels of the New Testament is the greatest story of all time. The gospels tell the story of Jesus, the Savior of the world. He was born to a virgin mother, whom the Holy Spirit impregnated. During His lifetime, Jesus chose twelve disciples who would walk alongside Him during His tenure on earth. For Jesus's story to be shared throughout the ages, God anointed four writers. We know them today as Matthew, Mark, Luke, and John. The first three tell a very similar story of the journey of Jesus, and their writing is referred to as the Synoptic Gospels. John, the fourth gospel story, is consistent with the truths of the Synoptic Gospels, but he shares Jesus's journey with a slightly different lens.

Jesus's spiritual biography takes precedence over all the stories of the human race. Even though all the books in the world cannot contain His full story, the writings that we are given are adequate for readers to understand His soul journey.

Below, please note a few pertinent facts about His life:

- He was fully God and fully man.
- He is known as the second person of the Trinity.
- His mother, Mary, was impregnated by the Holy Spirit.
- He was a carpenter's son.

- He was born in Bethlehem (which means house of bread).
- He was a student of God's Holy Word.
- He was a single man.
- He started His ministry around the age of thirty.
- His prayer in John 17 is noted as His longest prayer.
- While on earth, He ministered for about three and a half years.
- He was a miracle-working God, performing thirty-seven miracles.
- He was persecuted.
- He hung on a cross from approximately 9:00 a.m. until 3:00 p.m. This is a total of six hours.
- He died on an old, rugged cross.
- His story is the greatest story ever told.

The seven last words of Jesus on the cross were:

1. "*Eli, Eli, lema sabachthani?*" (which means "My God, my God, why have you forsaken me?"). (Matthew 27:46)
2. "Father, forgive them, for they do not know what they are doing." (Luke 23:34)
3. "Truly I tell you, today you will be with me in paradise." (Luke 23:43)
4. "'Woman, here is your son,' and to the disciple, 'Here is your mother.'" (John 19:26–27)
5. "I am thirsty." (John 19:28)
6. "It is finished." (John 19:30)
7. "Father, into your hands I commit my spirit." (Luke 23:46)

One of the most quoted texts that adequately summarizes the life of Jesus is the Apostle's Creed. I was raised in the Baptist church, and my husband grew up in the African Methodist Episcopal (AME) church. After fourteen years of marriage, we attended an AME church in Rochester Hills, Michigan. It was at this church that I learned the Apostle's Creed. It reads:

> I believe in God the Father Almighty, Maker of heaven and earth, and in Jesus Christ his only Son our Lord who was conceived by the Holy Spirit, born of the Virgin Mary, suffered under Pontius Pilate, was crucified, dead; and buried. The third day he arose from the dead, he ascended into heaven and sitteth at the right hand of God the Father Almighty; from thence he shall come to judge the quick and the dead. I believe in the Holy Spirit, the Church Universal, the communion of saints, the forgiveness of sins, the resurrection of the body and the life everlasting. Amen.[3]

Paul's Journey

The apostle Paul contributed some two-thirds of the New Testament. He writes from his late thirties to his sixties. His authentic epistles are considered Galatians, Romans, 1 Corinthians, 2 Corinthians, Philemon, Philippians, and 1 Thessalonians. This set of epistles is noted to have been written between 50 and 58 CE. The three epistles that scholars are evenly divided on, as they relate to his authenticity as the writer, are 2 Thessalonians, Colossians, and Ephesians. Additional epistles accredited to having been written by the apostle are 1 and 2 Timothy and Titus. Some scholars identified these last three letters as pseudepigraphic (written by someone other than the credited author) and were written a decade later. However, most scholars believe that the apostle wrote thirteen epistles. One of the most significant questions regards the authorship of the book of Hebrews. And undoubtedly, the authenticity of this book brings the vague possibility of the apostle's writing to fourteen books. Still, most historical critics do not attribute this book to Pauline authorship.

Regardless of the technicality as it relates to the authenticity of the authorship of the Pauline Epistles, the apostle Paul has made a tremendous impact in Christendom. Not only have his letters provided spiritual guidance over the centuries, but they also reveal how the power of God's Spirit transformed Paul's spiritual journey. His journey provides insight into the vicissitudes of real life and real time. In so many ways, you and I can relate to the apostle. Often, we can actually see characteristics of ourselves in his life. The following are a few high points of his life, spanning 50–60 CE. I pray that they are helpful for you as you see the reality of life that is revealed through Paul's story.

- He was a student of the Word.
- He studied under Rabbi Gamaliel. (Rabbi Gamaliel was a member of the Sanhedrin at age sixteen.)
- Before his salvation, Paul was a persecutor of believers.
- He experienced Jesus firsthand on a road called Damascus.
- He lived with an ailment.
- It was referred to as "a thorn" in his flesh.
- Its purpose was to buffet him.

- He was persecuted for his faith (belief) in the Lord Jesus Christ.
- He died a martyr's death.

As we look at Paul's story, it's helpful to turn our attention to 2 Corinthians.

> Second Corinthians may be considered as an autobiography of the Apostle Paul. In it we see a portrait of a person who lived in the Spirit. For us to enjoy and experience Christ in a rich way we must be persons in the Spirit as symbolized by ten aspects in 2 Corinthians—captives, letters, mirrors, vessels, ambassadors, co-workers, a temple, a virgin, lovers of the church, and tasters of Christ. It is by all of these aspects that we can be thoroughly wrought by God and with God and be constituted the ministers of the new covenant for the building up of the church.[4]

"Our sufficiency is from God, who has made us sufficient to be ministers of a new covenant, not of the letter but of the Spirit. For the letter kills, but the Spirit gives life" (2 Corinthians 3:5–6 ESV). This passage is befitting for a book that focuses on writing one's autobiography. The Spirit gives an individual life, and with life comes experiences. The experiences of life are the elements that make up the composition of a spiritual autobiography.

But 2 Corinthians also reveals the necessity to undergird one's spiritual autobiography with biblical references. The purpose of writing about one's journey is not merely personal but "for the building up of the church" to the glory of God. Understanding your journey is a transformative spiritual tool that equips you to be more effective in the kingdom of God. The prayer is that your journey will be the "portrait of a person who lived in the Spirit."

My sisters and brothers, the better you reflect and understand God's wisdom in the uniqueness of your journey, the more you will become a healthy asset in the body of Christ. I trust that you take the writing of your spiritual autobiography seriously as you seek to connect with God's activity in your past and as the Spirit transforms your present. To God be all the glory!

SELAH MOMENTS

PAUSING—Take a few deep breaths as you pause and think about what you have learned in this chapter about the biblical foundation for a spiritual autobiography.

REFLECTING—Reflect on your intake and how you sense God is speaking directly to you based on your insight into Jesus's and Paul's journeys.

PRAYING—Pray about how Paul's and Jesus's journeys may apply specifically to your spiritual journey. How does your life align with theirs? How is your journey different?

WRITING—Even now, you are spiritually, mentally, and emotionally preparing to write your spiritual autobiography as you reflect on the blessings of a biblical foundation for your writing. Make note of anything you would like to include.

Chapter 5

HISTORY OF A SPIRITUAL AUTOBIOGRAPHY

Before I formed you in the womb I knew you, before you were born I set you apart; I appointed you as a prophet to the nations.

Jeremiah 1:5

Writing a spiritual autobiography is not a new phenomenon. Throughout history, ministers, leaders, laity, historians, and people like you and me have put pen to paper and fingers to keyboards to tell their stories. A foundation for this transformative document began thousands of years ago.

Third-Century Story

"Although the foundations for the modern form of spiritual autobiography can be attributed to Saint Paul in the New Testament, the most significant figure in its evolution is Saint Augustine."[1] The first published spiritual autobiography was written by Saint Augustine (354–430), a Northern African Bishop. Like you and I, he did not live a perfect life. In Saint Augustine's book *Confessions*, he says that "he was a great sinner who became a great saint."[2] In this book, Augustine describes how God rescued him from his wayward life, false beliefs, and self-destructive behavior. He was not always living a holy life. He did not live a life with a commitment to the Lord until he was thirty-two years old.

Previously, we looked at Psalm 139, in which the psalmist was aware of God's activity in his life before he was born. Likewise, Augustine reflected on his journey with God from the early stages of his life. He writes, "You, O Lord God, gave me my life and my body when I was born. You gave my body its five senses; you furnished it with limbs and gave it its proper proportions; and you implanted it with all the instincts necessary for the welfare and safety of a living creature."[3] Saint Augustine was aware of his fallibility as a human being. He was also keenly aware of God's activity in his life from the beginning of his journey.

In *Confessions*, Augustine presents himself to the reader as the object of God's grace. "His life is not interesting as such but is the place where God's grace operates. God's grace in Augustine's life is not limited to information and help, rather it is a deep and direct influence of God on the most internal part of one's soul."[4] His life exemplifies the sufficiency of God's amazing grace.

Throughout Christendom, the concept of grace is a huge theme. Traditionally, we say that grace is God's unmerited favor. Augustine was a recipient who was fully attended by God's unmerited favor. Such favor cannot be gained but is granted by Yahweh Himself and no one else. No human being qualifies to grant this supernatural favor. God's grace is open to all. He will flood the gates of our soul as we open our souls to be the recipient of His supernatural grace.

Over the centuries, grace has been an incorporated theme that individuals are cognizant of as they write their spiritual autobiography. Grace is the spiritual ingredient that all souls need on their journey. Saint Augustine of Hippo has humbly postured and steeped himself in the acknowledgment of God's amazing grace. Consequently, Augustine has provided us with a solid foundation that exemplifies the need to embrace God's grace, operative when writing about one's story. Others have gleaned from his wisdom, have grasped this theology of grace, and have incorporated this God-given gift into their stories.

Seventeenth-Century Stories

John Bunyan

In 1666, an English Puritan preacher named John Bunyan wrote a book entitled *Grace Abounding to the Chief of Sinners: A Brief Account of God's Exceeding Mercy Through Christ to His Poor Servant*. Like Paul and Saint Augustine, Bunyan knew how God's grace was extended to him. Also like both authors, he was mindful of the sinful ways he lived before his conversion experience.

When wrestling with God's Word, Bunyan humbled himself and prayed:

> "Oh, Lord, I am a fool and not able to know the truth from error. Lord, leave me not to my own blindness, either to approve of or to condemn this doctrine. If it is of You, let me not despise it; if it is of the devil, let me not embrace it. Lord, I lay my soul in this matter at your feet. Let me not be deceived, I humbly ask You."[5]

Bunyan knew that without God's grace, he could not even discern right from wrong. In this quote, he humbly pleads for God's unmerited favor.

Monks

Monks were also known for writing spiritual autobiographies. In the seventeenth century, monks wrote spiritual autobiographies stimulated by their need to give personal testimony to become church members. They would often write about the sins they committed during their youth. As they matured in their faith, they would encounter a spiritual awakening, leading them to repent of their sin. After they repented, they would often sin again and then repent again, repeating the process. Such a cyclical pattern could occur several times for several years. Regardless of the number of times they sinned, they would seek God's "exceedingly abundant"[6] grace and forgiveness.

Throughout the century, thousands of ordinary women and men had conversion experiences. Likewise, they implemented the discipline of writing their spiritual autobiographies in an effort to better comprehend God's activity in their lives.

D. Bruce Hindmarsh, a professor at Regent College in Vancouver, wrote *The Evangelical Conversion Narrative: Spiritual Autobiography in Early Modern England*. In his book, Hindmarsh indicates the journey of pastors, leaders, laity, women and men, and Western and non-Western believers during the seventeenth century. His intent in writing this book was to reinforce the impact of sharing one's story. The expected outcome was verified in how individuals indicated that they had found wisdom and insight as they wrote their spiritual autobiographies.

During their reflections, a cyclical receptive pattern evolved. The cycle included the sharing of one's

- sin during their youth
- spiritual awakening

- anxiety as they reflected on the state of their soul
- repentance of their sin
- backsliding into sin
- comfort from God through His Word
- repetition of the cycle all over again

Throughout their journey, individuals would come to the full realization of the manifestation of the gracious gift of God's unconditional love that was expressed through their personal encounters with His eternal salvation.

Vavasor Powell

Other seventeenth-century narratives include that of the Welsh evangelistic preacher Vavasor Powell (1617–1670). Powell wrote *Spiritual Experiences of Sundry Believers*, a book containing testimonies from gathered churches in the United Kingdom. Powell, along with hundreds of other Christians in Wales and England, wrote a testimony against wickedness in high places. One passage that references such wickedness is found in Ephesians 6:12.[7]

Along with others, Powell was aware of the forces of evil present in the life of the believer. It is because of God's grace that each of us is empowered and equipped to endure the journey that is set before us. Each autobiography will have evil components. These, too, are a part of the testimony and are pivotal dots on the journey.

Nineteenth- and Twentieth-Century Stories

Thérèse of Lisieux

One of my favorite books is The *Story of a Soul: The Autobiography of Thérèse of Lisieux*. Thérèse of Lisieux (January 2, 1873–September 30, 1897) was a French

Discalced Carmelite.[8] During her lifetime, she had several other names, including:

- Saint Thérèse of the Child Jesus and the Holy Face
- Thérèse de l'Enfant Jésus et de la Sainte Face (French)
- The Little Flower of Jesus
- The Little Flower
- La Petite Thérèse

In the classical autobiography of Thérèse of Lisieux, she shares her deep love for God regardless of the adversities she encountered. Even amid sickness and disease, her heart was drawn closer to Yahweh. Unlike many of us who struggle with pain and suffering, she felt that such situations drew her closer to the lover of her very soul. It is challenging to imagine that this young lady had such depth of wisdom. She was infinitely passionate about her relationship with her God. She overtly expressed her love for Jesus. At the early age of fifteen, she joined the Carmelites in Lisieux, Normandy.

When I entered the first residency at Gordon-Conwell Theological Seminary in September 2009, *The Story of a Soul: The Autobiography of Thérèse of Lisieux* was the book that my professor, Dr. David Currie, recommended that I read. This was not a book that I would normally gravitate toward. However, as I read every page, I increasingly befriended my dear sister Thérèse. Even though I never met her, I realized we were sisters in the Spirit. We both loved our Lord and Savior, Jesus Christ. We both knew what it felt like to endure excruciating pain and sickness.

During my intense mitral valve prolapse heart surgery in January 2014, when pain became unbearable, I reflected on how Thérèse of Lisieux endured excruciating agony during her sickness. Her pain drew her closer to Yahweh. As her words came to my mind, God's grace enabled me to endure as I embraced her philosophy. Like St. Thérèse, I clung closer to the Lord when no pill could soothe me.

Often, when we suffer, we do not immediately see the benefits of suffering. It is not our innate human nature to embrace times of pain and suffering. While in agony, our first instinct is not to think that such situations are designed for us to develop deeper intimacy with Yahweh.

I believe that Thérèse of Lisieux's relationship with Yahweh, and the pain she endured, equipped her to connect the dots of the activity of God during her most challenging hours. Truly her life exemplifies a *Soul Journey* that transformed her present by discovering God throughout her life. Stories like hers and those of biblical saints and other formative leaders provide paradigms or good models for writing spiritual autobiographies.

Dr. Howard Thurman

Let us now look at the twentieth-century Christian mystic Dr. Howard Thurman, a world-renowned African American philosopher and author of *With Head and Heart: The Autobiography of Howard Thurman.*[9] This book's nine informative chapters provide readers with an overview of Thurman's childhood through his adult years.

As a professor, he taught students about the necessity of knowing themselves. His quest to understand himself equipped him to encourage others to do the same.

Early in Thurman's life, he was well acquainted with the spirit of racism, injustices, and religiosity that penetrated his culture. Such unfortunate exposures shaped his mindset and instilled in him a tenacious determination not to be a product of such behavior.

At the age of seven, a young Thurman faced harsh

realities when his father, Saul Solomon Thurman, died. The white undertaker refused to embalm his father, and the local church pastor refused to eulogize his father because he was not a member of the congregation. This indignant behavior impacted Thurman to the extent that he vowed never to be involved in the church's ministry.

During the family's grieving, a traveling preacher agreed to eulogize Thurman's father. To much dismay, the preacher used the service to spread his evangelistic agenda and to preach the deceased into hell. These incidents shaped Thurman's theology. Despite the racist and religious spirits he encountered, Thurman felt compelled to accept his call to serve Holy God. His yes to God was a yes that God used to develop him into a spiritual leader, preacher, teacher, chaplain, and dean.

He served as chaplain at Morehouse and Spelman Universities in Atlanta, Georgia. In addition, he served as Dean of Chapel at Howard University, Washington, DC, and Boston College in Massachusetts. As a pastor, Thurman served at Mount Zion Baptist Church (1926–1928) in Oberlin, Ohio, and later as co-pastor at The Church for the Fellowship in San Francisco, California. This church was first organized and founded in 1944. Its founders were Dr. Howard Thurman and Dr. Alfred Fisk. This congregation was identified as the first interracial congregation and the first interfaith congregation that was founded in the United States of America.

Because of Thurman's relationship with Jesus, he refused to allow the pain of the past to determine his assignment in the kingdom of God. He understood that life comes with highs and lows. Not only is Jesus present during the good season, but He is also present during the more challenging season. Thurman understood that Jesus would never leave him nor forsake him (Deuteronomy 31:8).

Thurman did not allow the sour days to overshadow the sweet days God had in store for him. Even though his heart was broken for a season, he used that season as a catapulting force for the kingdom of God. May we all be encouraged by his story.

From all of the above stories, we see that documenting our life's testimony is a great, faith-filled discipline. It is a good idea to have your documentation supported by Scripture. One scripture that relates to sharing our testimonies is found in the book of Revelation. John the Revelator writes, "They triumphed over him by the blood of the Lamb and by the word of their testimony" (Revelation 12:11). The testimony of each person's life is a witnessing tool to another.

In 2012, Oxford University Press published *Protestant Autobiography in the Seventeenth-Century Anglophone World*. In this book, Dr. Kathleen Lynch shares testimonies of members of English and American churches during the seventeenth century.

Lynch finds tremendous value in the testimony of Saint Augustine of Hippo's *Confessions*. In her book, she shares how Augustine impacted seventeenth-century formation leaders as they embarked upon reflecting and writing about their personal spiritual experiences. Lynch notes the significance of an individual's documentation prior to their becoming assimilated into the faith community. This is a part of their spiritual journey that should be noted as a necessary documentation alongside the confession of faith and baptism. Often, as we write our spiritual autobiography, we seek to omit what happened before we develop a personal relationship with Christ. However, documentation of our journey is significant when connecting the dots of our lives and rediscovering our pasts.

Dr. Lynch takes a look at the history of persons writing their spiritual autobiographies and expresses the blessings of reading about others' testimonies. One article summarizes her conclusions:

> Worshippers' testimonies were widely discussed and sometimes published in collections of "experiences" designed to further the spread and influence of particular ministers and congregations, or to testify to the (partial) successes of American colonists in managing their own religious affairs and converting the indigenous peoples they encountered in the Americas. This makes spiritual "experiences" unusual—and thought-provoking—as autobiographical texts.[10]

SELAH MOMENTS

PAUSING—Take a few deep breaths as you pause and think about what you have learned in chapter 5. What is surfacing in your mind?

REFLECTING—Reflect on your intake and how God is speaking directly to you through your readings about the history of a spiritual autobiography. Which spiritual leader do you most identify with and why? Which do you identify with the least, and why?

PRAYING—Pray about how these leaders' journeys impact yours as you begin to write your story, which will impact you and others.

WRITING—Continue to prepare yourself spiritually, mentally, and emotionally for the writing of your story. Keep notes about what you want to say or explore.

Chapter 6

THE EPIPHANY OF SEEING THE STAR

When they saw the star, they were overjoyed.
Matthew 2:10

You and I cannot turn back the hands of time; however, reflecting on the journey of our past can be rewarding. It can help us rediscover God in our past. And, thinking about what you would say to your younger self can be beneficial. As you mature, there are lessons you learned along the way. Many times, if you were given the chance to do life again, perhaps you would respond to it differently.

Several years ago, I was invited to speak at Gordon-Conwell Theological Seminary on "What I Would Say to My Younger Self." This was so much fun. However, to speak to my younger self, I had to give myself permission to reminisce on the past without trying to fix anything. The past is just that. It is the *past*. As I looked into the rearview mirror of my life, I began to notice the plethora of hats that I had worn over the years. Some of this information will seem like a repeat of previous chapters, but it is meant to show you my reflections and hopefully inspire your own.

As a young person, I was a student and worked on the farm. At the age of fourteen, I began my country retail career of sewing for profit and selling candy to the local farm workers. At the age of sixteen, I started spending the summers with my older sister, Permella (Pam), in Philadelphia. While there, I worked in a cafeteria and with a bookbinding company. Upon graduation from college, I began my career in retail and fashion.

At twenty-five, I married the love of my life, Gilbert L. Peacock. To this union, God blessed us with a lovely daughter. (My husband named her Vérnee Ivy Peacock. She is a V.I.P.) During this part of my life, my main focus was on my family. However, I was able to work in retail in Manhattan, and I opened a boutique with a partner.

In my early forties, I accepted my call into the ministry and attended Princeton Theological Seminary. Afterwards, I served in full-time ministry. In 2013, I graduated with my doctorate from Gordon-Conwell Theological Seminary. For sure the story continues and continues and continues. I just say I have worn numerous hats and through a myriad of experiences, God has blessed me with tremendous insight and stories to share with my younger self.

I shared a portion of my younger-self story in chapter 2. I plan to write my full spiritual autobiography one day in the near future. With the numerous hats that I have worn over the years, I would say to my younger self, "You were willing to take chances. However, there were many phases in your life that you could have believed in yourself much more. Yes, there were numerous times that you pressed through. Sometimes the press caused you to stay in places and spaces longer than you should have, but the grace of the Lord kept you regardless of the adversity. Truly, God has been good to you." And for that, I give Him praise!

At this juncture of your reading and perhaps writing, I ask you the same thing that I just did: What would you like to say to your younger self? Ponder that thought for a moment without getting bogged down, critical, or regretful. The good news is that you are living and you now have the opportunity to tell someone your story.

As you continue to connect the dots of your journey to transform your present, I encourage you to see your life on earth in stages that are identified by a concept called the Epiphany Journey. Epiphany was recognized as a feast day in the early church. In Greek, the word *epiphanies* means appearing. Epiphany celebrates Jesus's presence in the world. In the book of Matthew, we find the story of the wise men traveling to welcome the Christ King into the world. On their way to visit the Messiah, they encountered various steps.

They started in a dark space as they set out to see the Christ King. Ahead of them was a bright North Star that pointed them in the direction of their destination. Upon their arrival in Bethlehem, they presented the Christ King with gifts of gold, frankincense, and myrrh. We find this biblical story in the first gospel.

> After Jesus was born in Bethlehem in Judea, during the time of King Herod, Magi from the east came to Jerusalem and asked, "Where is the one who has been born king of the Jews? We saw his star when it rose and have come to worship him."
>
> When King Herod heard this he was disturbed, and all Jerusalem with him. When he had called together all the people's chief

priests and teachers of the law, he asked them where the Messiah was to be born. "In Bethlehem in Judea," they replied, "for this is what the prophet has written:

'But you, Bethlehem, in the land of Judah,
are by no means least among the rulers of Judah;
for out of you will come a ruler
who will shepherd my people Israel.'"

Then Herod called the Magi secretly and found out from them the exact time the star had appeared. He sent them to Bethlehem and said, "Go and search carefully for the child. As soon as you find him, report to me, so that I too may go and worship him."

After they had heard the king, they went on their way, and the star they had seen when it rose went ahead of them until it stopped over the place where the child was. When they saw the star, they were overjoyed. On coming to the house, they saw the child with his mother Mary, and they bowed down and worshiped him. Then they opened their treasures and presented him with gifts of gold, frankincense and myrrh. And having been warned in a dream not to go back to Herod, they returned to their country by another route. (Matthew 2:1–12)

The story of the Magi is the story of their pilgrimage as they sought to lay their eyes on King Jesus. Even though their journey began in the ambiguity of darkness, their hope remained. They eagerly kept searching for the shining star as a guide to their sacred destination. Such a journey requires one to be willing to leave the familiar with the anticipation of arriving in a God-ordained place. This kind of journey requires the desire to seek something you do not fully understand as you prayerfully believe that God has a revelation to unveil. This journey requires leaving the familiar as you seek new ways of being more fully present with God's activity.

Nine Epiphany Elements

Like the Magi, we must learn several lessons as we are on our epiphany journeys. Below are some comprehensive steps that took place with the Magi, and similar patterns will also occur on your pilgrimage. As you review the nine epiphany elements below, you will notice spiritual development and maturity. These epiphany elements will provide you with a unique understanding of the cycle of life. These elements are designed to be conduits that aid you in viewing your spiritual journey as one that is distinctively crafted by God, just for you.

1. Recognize your calling while waiting in the darkness.
   - Settle into your uncertainty.
   - Pause and reflect.
   - Ask, *Where do I sense God calling me?*
   - Ask, *Am I sensing any restlessness as I discern God tugging on my heart?*
2. More closely seek the Spirit's direction as you search the night star.
   - Scan the spiritual night sky as you seek guidance.
   - Where is the Holy Spirit directing you?

- What is He teaching you about the importance of connecting the dots of your journey?

3. Be vulnerable as you seek clarity from the star.
    - Follow the light as you identify your purpose.
    - Be willing to move forward even during times of uncertainty.
    - Notice what you are fearful of as you move forward.
4. Be tenacious in pressing forward on your journey.
    - Move forward in a Spirit-led direction.
    - See challenges as an opportunity to grow.
    - Notice your spiritual stamina, even when moving and pressing forward is challenging.
5. Seek God's revelation as you follow the star.
    - Continue your journey with persistence and perseverance.
    - Notice how God's wisdom is with you.
    - What opportunities are you encountering?
6. Celebrate your God-gifted story.
    - Embrace God's gift(s) in you.
    - Acknowledge and be thankful for your blessings.
    - What are you learning about yourself, and where are you sensing transformation?
7. Experience a new place.
    - Enter into your new space and place.
    - Find assurance in your destined accomplishments.
    - Acknowledge how the Spirit has kept you.
8. Share and apply your story.
    - Share your gifts, wisdom, knowledge, and revelation with others.

- Share lessons learned and commit to share more effectively with others.
- Remember, you cannot go back the way you have come. God is doing a new thing in you (Matthew 2:11–12).

9. Go a different route.
   - Acknowledge the new direction of the Spirit.
   - Realize that obedience is essential to walking into your new destiny.
   - Notice that others will be blessed by your sensitivity to the new direction.

As you and I seek to better understand the epiphany of life, we can learn about life and the most important relationship therein from the French Christian monk Brother Lawrence. Studying the life of Brother Lawrence will help us save ourselves a lot of trouble as we seek to prioritize who is most important in our lives. In his book *The Practice of the Presence of God the Best Rule of a Holy Life*, he shares that in his spiritual life, he desired to give himself "wholly to God." He continues,

> That God might take away my sin, *I renounced, for the love of Him, everything that was not He; and I began to live as if there was none but He and I in the world.* Sometimes I considered myself before Him as a poor criminal at the feet of his judge; at other times I beheld Him in my heart as my Father, as my God: I worshipped Him the oftenest that I could, keeping my mind in His holy Presence, and recalling it as often as I found it wandered from Him.[1]

Brother Lawrence kept his heart and mind in the right direction as he sought to abide in God's presence on his journey. His focus always leaned toward the North Star of God's presence.

For Those Who Have Far to Travel: An Epiphany Blessing

If you could see
the journey whole,
you might never
undertake it,
might never dare
the first step
that propels you
from the place
you have known
toward the place
you know not.
Call it
one of the mercies
of the road:
that we see it
only by stages
as it opens
before us,
as it comes into
our keeping,
step by
single step.
There is nothing
for it
but to go,
and by our going

take the vows
the pilgrim takes:
to be faithful to
the next step;
to rely on more
than the map;
to heed the signposts
of intuition and dream;
to follow the star
that only you
will recognize;
to keep an open eye
for the wonders that
attend the path;
to press on
beyond distractions,
beyond fatigue,
beyond what would
tempt you
from the way.
There are vows
that only you
will know:
the secret promises
for your particular path
and the new ones
you will need to make
when the road
is revealed
by turns
you could not
have foreseen.
Keep them, break them,
make them again;

each promise becomes
part of the path,
each choice creates
the road
that will take you
to the place
where at last
you will kneel
to offer the gift
most needed—
the gift that only you
can give—before turning to go home by
another way.[2]

SELAH MOMENTS

PAUSING—Take a few deep breaths as you pause and think about what you learned in chapter 6. What is surfacing in your mind?

REFLECTING—Reflect on your intake and how God is speaking directly to you through your reading about the Epiphany Journey.

PRAYING—Pray about lessons learned on your journey. Release things you wish you could change and embrace the good.

WRITING—Continue to prepare yourself spiritually, mentally, and emotionally as you write notes about your journey.

Chapter 7

YOUR ESCHATOLOGICAL LIFE

There will be no more night. They will not need the light of a lamp or the light of the sun, for the Lord God will give them light. And they will reign for ever and ever.

Revelation 22:5

The ultimate purpose of writing your spiritual autobiography is to see the hand of God throughout the course of your life and to anticipate eternal life with Jesus Christ. The more you and I understand our ultimate purpose in Christ, the more we will understand the complexity of our spiritual journey. Writing your story will better equip you to live more effectively day-to-day as you seek to fulfill your God-given kingdom assignment. The more you can comprehend, embrace, and connect the dots on your journey, whether good or challenging, the more at ease you will become in accepting God's perfect will and plan for your finite life. You can rediscover God in your past to help transform your present and point you toward your future. Thanks be to God, your finiteness here on earth does not determine the infiniteness of your soul.

In 2023, I had the pleasure of meeting Dr. Gary Moon at Richmont Theological Seminary in Atlanta, Georgia. Both of us taught a class during the gathering of the doctoral students' cohort. During my time with Gary and his wife, Regina, he was kind enough to bless me with a signed copy of his newest book, *Becoming Dallas Willard*. What a jewel! I will treasure this book forever.

In Moon's book, he shares a letter that Willard wrote to his wife, Jane. Moon denotes how Willard was maturing in his faith and became more aware of his past and present. Willard wrote to his wife: "We must understand how love, joy, and peace can be our portion in every state of life and can lead us into a radiant eternity with God."[1] Such spiritual attributes provide supernatural spiritual nourishment for the soul on earth as well as in eternity. The apostle Paul says it best to the church at Philippi: "I press on toward the goal to win the prize for which God has called me heavenward in Christ Jesus" (Philippians 3:14).

Even though your journey here on earth will cease, God has a heavenly journey in store for you. The finiteness of this heavenward account has not yet been revealed. "Our years will all be complete only when they have all moved into the past."[2] Currently, we just see through a glass dimly, but one day we will see Him face-to-face. One day we will journey eternally in our heavenly home. In that place, there is no more dying or death, for the Lord himself "'will wipe every tear from their eyes. There will be no more death' or mourning or crying or pain, for the old order of things has passed away" (Revelation 21:4). This is the final part of your story that has yet to be written. Selah.

On Sunday, December 8, 2024, I could not wait to join The Park Church's adult Sunday school class. This Zoom session was on fire! The teacher for the day was Edith Brown, and there were seventeen attendees online. The lesson was on Ecclesiastes 3:1–8, 14–15. One student in this class was Minister Viness Warren. During the time of discussion, she noted that in 2019, I preached a sermon titled "These Are the Days of Our Life." I was totally shocked when she said that. Minister Warren informed us that it was her tradition to make a notation in her Bible of the text, date, and preacher of a specified scripture. That had been five years ago.

This Sunday school lesson pierced my heart as I quietly reflected on the fragility of life. As we read the book of Ecclesiastes, we find a multiplicity of meanings for life. Historians attribute the authorship of Ecclesiastes to King Solomon, who is affectionally known as the Preacher. In chapters 1–2, King Solomon notes how all in life is vanity. How life is merely folly. In chapter 3, he breaks down life's experiences and identifies twenty-eight encounters, including birthing, dying, planting, plucking, killing, healing, breaking down, building up, weeping, laughing, mourning, dancing, casting away stones, gathering stones, embracing, refraining from embracing, getting, losing, keeping, casting away, rending, sewing, keeping silent, speaking, loving, hating, and lastly, making war and peace. No one on this side of heaven who lives any length of time will live life and not encounter similar experiences. In all of these encounters, God remains sovereign and in control.

As you can imagine, after class, I could not wait to find the sermon from 2019. Here are two paragraphs from my sermon that I would like to share with you.

> God wants us to know that there is a time, a place, and a season for everything. He wants us to know that troubles don't last always. He wants us to know that weeping may endure for a night but joy comes in the morning. He wants us to know that regardless of what you may be going through,

> all things still work together for good to those who love the Lord and to those who are called according to His purpose. The good is the birthing. The good is the healing, the laughing, the dancing, and the birthing.
>
> So, celebrate the birthing, because God saw fit to bring you into this world some years ago. Celebrate the healing, because you do not look like what you've been through. Celebrate the laughing, because what the enemy thought would take you out did not. Celebrate the dancing, because when you think about Jesus and all He has done for you, you could dance, dance, dance, dance all night.[3]

Before the celebration at the end of my sermon, I closed with the song, "I Won't Complain" by Rev. Paul Jones.[4] The song talks about good and bad days but acknowledges that God has been good in the midst of all of those days.

During our Sunday school class, in addition to the biblical text for the day, another scripture was highlighted by a dear friend, Minister Steward Ralph. I have known him for over three decades, and his passion for God's Word is always evident whether he is preaching, teaching, praying, or just having a general conversation. The scripture Minister Ralph quoted was, "Therefore we do not lose heart. Though outwardly we are wasting away, yet inwardly we are being renewed day by day" (2 Corinthians 4:16). At first, my question was, "How does this passage connect with the Sunday school lesson?"

During the teaching, I kept meditating on the verse

and asked God to show me how it connected. I admit, I checked out for a moment. As I sat with the passage, God began to show me a worn, cracked, and tattered shoe that had holes in it. The exterior was well worn, while the smooth and shiny interior, bright red leather lining, was brand-new (like the smoothness of a new pair of popular ladies' red-bottom shoes). I grasped this concept, but God had more to show me. I began to visualize how aging can cause one to become crippled, sick, or suffering from an incurable disease. Such calamities cause the body to waste away. Even with such devastating exterior debilitation, the soul is being renewed day by day. While the flesh is dying, the soul is internally regenerated. The soul is bursting with exhilarating life-giving exuberance beyond human comprehension. The Spirit of God is renewing the spirit of humanity while the flesh is "wasting away." As I reflected on the interior of the shoe, even the red leather would perish. Only the Spirit and the glory of God inside the shoe could keep it fresh. Likewise, the spirit within the soul of an individual, when it is ignited by the Holy Spirit, will reveal the glory of the Lord.

As we go through life's circumstances and encounter the days of our lives, the wear and tear of life will manifest its demise. Anything exterior that is fleshy will undoubtedly die. The dirt of our flesh must return to the dirt of the earth. Regardless of the pain and suffering that occur externally, the good news is that the soul, the inward person, is being renewed.

SELAH MOMENTS

PAUSING—Take a few deep breaths as you pause and think about what you have learned in chapter 7. What is surfacing in your mind?

REFLECTING—Reflect on your intake and how God is speaking directly through the readings about your life to come.

PRAYING—Pray about souls you know who need to invite Jesus into their story.

WRITING—You are now ready to begin the process of writing your story! Take some time to reflect on how you feel about writing your story.

Chapter 8

SPIRITUAL AUTOBIOGRAPHY WORKBOOK

"For I know the plans I have for you," declares the L*ORD*, *"plans to prosper you and not to harm you, plans to give you hope and a future."*

Jeremiah 29:11

This chapter is a workbook designed to provide an in-depth and detailed document of your story. It is about your life's story with God and seeing Him throughout every aspect of your soul journey. Feel free to start writing in the blanks provided, then continue in your own journal. After you write your spiritual autobiography, I hope you will be able to share it in a small group, and long term, I highly recommend that you share it with your spiritual director.[1] If you desire to teach *Soul Journey: Transform Your Present by Rediscovering God in Your Past* independently of our institute, Peacock Soul Care, see appendix 1: Teacher's Guide.[2]

This Workbook Belongs To

The date you began writing your spiritual autobiography

The date you finished writing your spiritual autobiography

The date you shared your spiritual autobiography in a group setting

---

The date you began sharing your spiritual autobiography with a spiritual director

---

Writing your spiritual autobiography is not some haphazard encounter. It requires intentionality as you seek to better understand the hand of God on your life from before birth until the very present moment of your current breath. It is one of the most transformative spiritual practices that you will experience.

The actual composition and components of your spiritual autobiography cover several areas. The sequence below will be beneficial as you embark upon this sacred and devoted writing. The components are:

- Praying
- Focusing
- Questioning
- Thinking
- Writing
- Journeying

Praying

As you begin to write your spiritual autobiography, you will notice the activity of God. You will see that "God is active in all lives at all times, but not all people notice—much less respond to God. To write a spiritual autobiography is to notice and noticing enables us to respond in new ways to God."[3]

Richard Peace, in his book *Spiritual Autobiography: Discovering and Sharing Your Spiritual Story*, provides a simple guideline for writing about one's journey. Below is a portion of Peace's checklist for dividing your life into various periods as you write your spiritual autobiography.[4]

1. Pray for God to remind you of different periods in your life. Pray for the Holy Spirit to help you recall

specific places, people, and experiences of each age period.

2. Pray for God to show you periods of high points. These will include times of celebration and pleasant memories.
3. Pray for God to show you periods of low points. These will include moments when you experience a crisis of faith, doubt, disobedience, seasons of darkness, depression, etc.
4. As you consider the circumstances above, seek to identify the outcomes of growth. Such growth will include maturation intellectually, emotionally, behaviorally, relationally, or simply growth in service.

Now that you have prayed and thought about such periods of your life, now is the time to begin your writing. As you write, notice God's movements in your life. As you start writing, consider if you will present your spiritual autobiography. The setting and guidelines for your presentation will determine the length of your sharing time.

As you write, you will begin to see a pattern, a process, and a rhythm in which God has guided your life. Implementing your spiritual autobiography is designed to competently equip you to experience a more in-depth understanding of your spiritual journey. To most effectively reap the benefits of writing such a document, I recommend that you bathe the implementation of this discipline in prayer. Your prayer focus may include the following concepts that are supported by Scripture:

- Your ability to see and comprehend how the plan of God has been working in your life.

  "For surely I know the plans I have for you, says the LORD, plans for your welfare and not for harm, to give you a future with hope" (Jeremiah 29:11 NRSV).

  "The LORD makes firm the steps of the one who delights in him" (Psalm 37:23).

- Your ability to have perfect memory allows you to recall spiritual benchmarks of your life.

  "But the Advocate, the Holy Spirit, whom the Father will send in my name, will teach you everything, and remind you of all that I have said to you" (John 14:26 NRSV).

  "Who has known the mind of the Lord so as to instruct him?" (1 Corinthians 2:16).

- Your ability to understand that God was still there even in the difficult times.

  "We know that all things work together for good for those who love God, who are called according to his purpose" (Romans 8:28 NRSV).

  "Be strong and courageous. Do not be afraid or terrified because of them, for the LORD your God goes with you; he will never leave you nor forsake you" (Deuteronomy 31:6).

- Your ability to see how God has led you on your journey up until this point in your life.

  "But as it is, God arranged the members in the body, each one of them, as he chose" (1 Corinthians 12:18 NRSV).

> "Trust in the LORD with all your heart and lean not on your own understanding; in all your ways submit to him, and he will make your paths straight" (Proverbs 3:5–6).

Begin writing here or in a separate journal what God has shown you through prayer.

Focusing

Focusing requires giving God your undivided attention. This is an act of worship that honors God's presence and His hand on your life. Remember the following things when writing about the stages of your life.

1. Always keep your focus on what God is saying and doing. As you begin, you may have some challenges recalling and bringing order to your document but remember that the Holy Spirit will give you perfect recall and identify all the information you need to include.
2. As you write, consider the time as sacred and as an act of reverential worship. All of God's activity in your life is part of your journey. It does not belong to anyone else. It consists of your DNA and unique rhythms.
3. On this journey, you will have times that you remember more vividly than others, and that is to be expected. In addition, you will have moments of memory where you may press in as you seek to recall more vividly.
4. Do not be afraid to zone in on the difficult moments and seasons. They may not be pretty, but the good news is you have lived to talk about them. Just remember each and every circumstance that you have encountered is significant and divine.
   - It is part of your journey.
   - God kept you through it.
   - He was there even when you felt all alone.
   - He was there even when you felt He was absent.

Begin writing here or in a separate journal what God has shown you through prayer.

Questioning

To question means to inquire or seek information that is beneficial for the speaking and the listening participant. When writing your story, asking the right questions is key. When a practical question is asked, the desired outcome is to obtain the necessary results. Here are some relevant questions to ask:

1. As you reflect on whether you are drawing closer or moving further away from the lover of your soul (the Lord Jesus Christ), ask yourself what makes you answer the way you did.
2. What are the main events that you have encountered over your lifetime?
3. Below are some of the significant celebrations that have occurred during your lifetime. Some celebrations may include
   - Birth
   - Marriage
   - Graduation
   - Employment

   Please note others that you have encountered.
4. What are some of the struggles that you have experienced in your lifetime?
5. What crises have you encountered?
   - Please note that it is essential that you are sincere.
   - Identify any faith, relational, financial, or emotional crises.
6. How did these situations affect your life in the past or in the present?

7. Where was the Holy Spirit during the pleasant and not-so-pleasant events?

Begin writing here or in a separate journal what God has shown you through prayer.

Thinking

Thinking requires directing one's mind toward a particular person or object, pausing and reflecting, clearing one's mind of clutter, and focusing on an objective or thought. By doing so, one engages and activates one's memory.

Saint Augustine writes that

> the memory is like a storehouse for countless images of all kinds which are conveyed to it by the senses. In it are stored away all thoughts by which we enlarge upon or diminish or modify in any way the perceptions at which we arrive through the senses, and it also contains anything else that has been entrusted to it for safe keeping.[5]

Time to Reflect

Reflection categories are below. Please take time to think on them as you begin to bring to memory relationships and events of the past. Before you dive deep into the membrane and recall the center of your mind, take time and graciously thank God for these precious and divine memories. Thank God for allowing you to reflect on your life with Him. Let us begin the reflection process.

1. Think about childhood experiences, such as first impressions, the conditions and surroundings of your upbringing, and persons who profoundly influenced your spirituality during your childhood. Share below.

2. See yourself as a young child with your parents, in your home or your school, or with a favorite teacher. What do you see?

3. Now come the teenage years, when there are many beginnings: the first date, the first kiss, and the first heartbreak. Share your firsts.

4. How did you feel when you became aware of changes in your body?

5. See yourself as a young adult with friends and colleagues. Bills now become part of your responsibility because the apron string has been cut. You are no longer a little girl or a little boy. How does this affect you?

6. As an adult, you have learned much about life and are still learning. What insights are you gaining? Is there a spiritual awakening?

7. During this season, you begin to establish practices, patterns, and rhythms that set the tone of your journey. What are you noticing?

8. Who have you identified as mentors, role models, and spiritual guides, and why?

9. Reflect on how you assimilated at your workplace and how you served in your church home. Share below.

10. See yourself at special moments of celebration and share below.
    - Graduation from

Kindergarten	High school
Middle school	College(s)

    - Sacred Time of

Conversion to Christ	Giving birth to children

11. Now, focus on significant transitions in your spiritual journey. Think about transitions from one job to another, transitions from one city or state to another, transitions in how you respond to events or people, etc. Write them below.

12. Think about those who influenced your spiritual growth. Such people may include your parents, grandparents, godparents, clergy, teachers, neighbors, friends, mentors, spiritual directors, counselors, etc. Share their names and influences below.

13. Share your physical moves and how these adjustments impacted you.

14. Write down career changes you have had over the decades.

15. What mental and emotional shifts have you had to make over the years?

16. Focus on the significant encounters of your spiritual journey that had a major impact on shaping who you are or are not. Write them below.

17. Who are some of the people who have stayed with you over the years, and who are the ones God caused you to separate from?

18. What belief systems have you adopted or separated from?

19. How has your spirituality impacted your journey?

Continue writing here or in a separate journal what God has shown you through prayer.

Writing

Your Entrance

Before you begin writing in this section, please allow me to assist you as you imagine being birthed into this world. Read the following slowly; feel free to reread as many times as you'd like.

On a particular day, you were born into this world. Your mother was either in a hospital or in another space. Regardless of the actual location, there was a moment when you were ready to enter the world. As you sit back in your chair, place your hands on your lap, center your mind, and slowly inhale and exhale. Once you are all settled in, imagine the day you were born. When you entered the world, you were separated from your birth mother. An umbilical cord was cut. You were wrapped in cloth. And you were given a name.

Perhaps it was just you, your mother, and an assistant in the birthing space, or there could have been others. As you keep your eyes closed, imagine who was in the room with you and your mom the day you were born. What were the expressions on their faces? What did they say? How did your mother feel when she first held you?

You may have other questions or reflections. Take your time and allow the Spirit to speak to you. Slow down, breathe, and just be. Now, we will continue the writing journey.

Telling Your Story

Writing your spiritual autobiography draws the pieces of your life puzzle and connects the dots. Unfortunately, most of the time we do not necessarily see God's hand on our lives before we are born. Jeremiah 1:4–5 (ESV) says, "Now the word of the LORD came to me, saying, 'Before I formed you in the womb I knew you, and before you were born, I consecrated you; I appointed you a prophet to the nations." This passage confirms that God knew you before you were born, consecrated you, and set you apart for a particular assignment in His kingdom.

Writing your spiritual autobiography is a call to see the Lord God working in your life. Such a document will be instrumental in your spiritual development and maturity.

When you write about your transformative journey, you will begin to see a pattern, a process, and a rhythm. The spiritual autobiography is designed to effectively equip you to experience a more in-depth understanding of your journey. As you begin to write, you will notice the activity of God. My prayer is that you see supernaturally as you dive into the crevices of your journey. I pray that you notice things, people, and events that you did not notice before. Consequently, you will see God's activity in your life with fresh lenses. So now let us begin the writing journey.

Journeying

Please fill in the blanks in the section below or use your own journal.

AGES ONE TO TWENTY
YOUR FIRST QUARTER OF LIFE

Your Story: One to Ten Years of Age

1. Identify the important people in your life.
2. From the ages of one to ten, what were your most memorable moments?
3. From the ages of one to ten, how did you see yourself?
4. Why did you identify the people you listed above as the most important people in your life?

5. Why did you identify the moment that you listed above as your most memorable moment?
6. Why did you see yourself the way you did?

Your Story: Eleven to Twenty Years of Age

1. From the ages of eleven to twenty, who were the most important people in your life?
2. From the ages of eleven to twenty, what were your most important decisions?
3. From the ages of eleven to twenty, what was the most memorable moment during that season of your life?
4. From the ages of eleven to twenty, what was your most pivotal moment?
5. Why did you consider this the most pivotal moment?
6. From the ages of eleven to twenty, how did you see yourself?
7. Why did you identify the people you listed above as the most important people in your life?
8. Why did you identify the decision that you listed above as the most important decision?
9. Why was the moment you indicated above the most memorable?

AGES TWENTY-ONE TO FORTY
YOUR SECOND QUARTER OF LIFE

Your Story: Twenty-One to Thirty Years of Age

1. From the ages of twenty-one to thirty, who were the most important people in your life?
2. From the ages of twenty-one to thirty, what were your most important decisions?
3. From the ages of twenty-one to thirty, what was the most memorable moment during that season of your life?
4. From the ages of twenty-one to thirty, what was your most pivotal moment? Please note why you considered this most pivotal.
5. From the ages of twenty-one to thirty, how did you see yourself? Describe who you considered yourself to be.
6. Why did you describe the people you listed above as the most important people in your life?
7. Why did you identify the decision that you listed above as the most important decision?
8. Why was the moment you indicated above the most memorable?

Your Story: Thirty-One to Forty Years of Age

1. From the ages of thirty-one to forty, who were the most important people in your life?
2. From the ages of thirty-one to forty, what were the most important decisions you made?
3. From the ages of thirty-one to forty, what was the most memorable moment during that season of your life?
4. From the ages of thirty-one to forty, how did you see yourself?
5. Why did you describe the people you listed above as the most important people in your life?
6. Why did you identify the decision that you listed above as the most important decision?
7. Why was the moment you indicated above the most memorable?
8. What crisis of belief did you encounter that required faith in action?

AGES FORTY-ONE TO SIXTY
YOUR THIRD QUARTER OF LIFE

Your Story: Forty-One to Fifty Years of Age

1. From the ages of forty-one to fifty, who were the most important people in your life?
2. From the ages of forty-one to fifty, what were the most important decisions you made?
3. From the ages of forty-one to fifty, what was the most memorable moment during that season of your life?
4. From the ages of forty-one to fifty, what was your most pivotal moment?
5. Why did you consider this the most pivotal moment?
6. Why did you describe the people you listed above as the most important people in your life?
7. Why did you identify the decision that you listed above as the most important decision?
8. Why was the moment you indicated above the most memorable?

Your Story: Fifty-One to Sixty Years of Age

1. From the ages of fifty-one to sixty, who were the most important people in your life?
2. From the ages of fifty-one to sixty, what were the most important decisions you made?
3. From the ages of fifty-one to sixty, what was the most memorable moment during that season of your life?
4. From the ages of fifty-one to sixty, what was your most pivotal moment? Please note why you considered this the most pivotal.
5. From the ages of fifty-one to sixty, how did you see yourself?
6. Why did you describe the people you listed above as the most important people in your life?
7. Why did you identify the decision that you listed above as the most important decision?
8. Why was the moment you indicated above the most memorable?

AGES SIXTY-ONE TO EIGHTY
YOUR FOURTH QUARTER OF LIFE

Your Story: Sixty-One to Seventy Years of Age

1. From the ages of sixty-one to seventy, who were the most important people in your life?
2. From the ages of sixty-one to seventy, what were the most important decisions you made?
3. From the ages of sixty-one to seventy, what was the most memorable moment during that season of your life?
4. From the ages of sixty-one to seventy, what was your most pivotal moment? Please note why you considered this the most pivotal.
5. From the ages of sixty-one to seventy, how did you see yourself?
6. Why did you identify the people you listed above as the most important people in your life?
7. Why did you identify the decision that you listed above as the most important decision?
8. Why was the moment you indicated above the most memorable?

Your Story: Seventy-One to Eighty Years of Age

1. From the ages of seventy-one to eighty, who were the most important people in your life?
2. From the ages of seventy-one to eighty, what were the most important decisions you made?
3. From the ages of seventy-one to eighty, what was the most memorable moment during that season of your life?
4. From the ages of seventy-one to eighty, what was your most pivotal moment? Please note why you considered this the most pivotal.
5. From the ages of seventy-one to eighty, how did you see yourself? Describe who you considered yourself to be.
6. Why did you describe the people you listed above as the most important people in your life?
7. Why did you identify the decision that you listed above as the most important decision?
8. Why was the moment you indicated above the most memorable?

BEYOND EIGHTY-ONE
YOUR BONUS QUARTER

1. Beyond the age of eighty-one, who are the most important people in your life?
2. Beyond the age of eighty-one, what are the most important decisions you have made?
3. Beyond the age of eighty-one, what has been the most memorable moment during this season of your life?
4. Beyond the age of eighty-one, what has been your most pivotal moment? Please note why you consider this the most pivotal.
5. Beyond the age of eighty-one, how do you see yourself? Describe who you consider yourself to be.
6. Why did you describe the people you listed above as the most important people in your life?
7. Why did you identify the decision that you listed above as the most important decision?
8. Why was the moment you indicated above the most memorable?

The importance of taking the time to write your story helps you to more effectively

- identify patterns on your journey
- see the hand of God on your life
- notice your life rhythm of ebbs and flows
- connect the dots of your life
- understand the specificity of your assignment in the kingdom of God
- see the Spirit's presence amidst the highs and lows as well as the good and challenging times (notice the word *bad* is not a choice for your journey), because it all works together for good (Romans 8:28).

After you have written and reflected on the bullets of the stages of your journey, you can now do some free writing prior to composing your final document.

Free Writing

This worshipful writing experience is a time of free writing. The concept of free writing is allowing your mind to reflect and wander without feeling burdened. Consider free writing from the outline you have written. It can be a helpful tool prior to the actual writing of your soul journey. Once your free writing is complete, you will be prepared to formally format your paper, project, book, etc. Please do not rush during this writing. You are setting a solid foundation for your story. After your free writing, it is now time to prepare to write an official document. After you complete your document, you are ready to share and present it. For writing, I recommend that it be:

- five to eight pages
- double spaced
- twelve-point font size
- Times New Roman font

Presenting

Now, it is time to present your paper. Be mindful that you will not be able to share everything, so prayerfully discern what you would like to share. You can share more in-depth with your spiritual director, mentor, coach, etc.

As you prepare to present to your colleagues in a small group or another chosen space, be your best authentic self as the Holy Spirit directs you on what to say. If you are reading this book individually, consider finding one or two trusted people you would like to share your story with and present it to them.

Continuing

Writing your spiritual autobiography is not a one-and-done process. God's imprint on your spiritual journey continues every day. Therefore, be encouraged as the pages of your life unfold themselves day by day, week by week, and month by month. Consider it an honor as you continue to explore the journey.

Do not allow the journey to become humdrum. As you continue on your spiritual journey, ask God to deepen your discernment, spiritual growth, and insights as you connect the dots of your amazing life.

As weeks, months, and years go by, continue to add to your story. Such inclusions will birth insights regarding God's hand in your life. Writing about your spiritual journey is a refreshing experience.

You may encounter a wall when writing your story. You may not feel inclined to write, or you may feel like there is nothing else to say. When you reach such a juncture, know that is a good time to be more intentional as you seek the Spirit's guidance. He will give you perfect recall and direction. Be mindful that the Holy Spirit is always speaking.

Noticing the activity of God or what seems like the lack thereof is part of your writing journey. As you write, take time to pause and see where the Holy Spirit is working.

SELAH MOMENTS

PAUSING —Take a few deep breaths as you pause and think about what you have learned in the process of writing your spiritual autobiography.

REFLECTING —Reflect on your intake and how God is speaking directly to you, based on your readings in chapter 8.

PRAYING —Pray about how the practice of writing about your soul journey aligns with other stories you have heard. Also, think about the uniqueness of your story. Now is a good time for a prayer of celebration for God's faithfulness in your life and your faithfulness to dive into writing about your journey. Well done!

CONCLUSION

There is a time for everything,
and a season for every activity
under the heavens:
a time to be born and a time to die,
a time to plant and a time to uproot,
a time to kill and a time to heal,
a time to tear down and a time to build,
a time to weep and a time to laugh,
a time to mourn and a time to dance,
a time to scatter stones and
a time to gather them,
a time to embrace and a time to
refrain from embracing,
a time to search and a time to give up,
a time to keep and a time to throw away,
a time to tear and a time to mend,
a time to be silent and a time to speak,
a time to love and a time to hate,
a time for war and a time for peace.

Ecclesiastes 3:1–8

Writing your spiritual autobiography takes time and requires you to empty the depths of your heart and to be willing to pour out your soul via paper, computer, or recording. In order for your soul to be attended to, there must be serious intentionality. Such a focus requires time and even a period of time away from the trappings of busyness.

Busy schedules continue to be a part of everyone's lives, so it would be a worthwhile venture to offer ongoing quarterly sessions with a focus on encouraging persons to continue their spiritual commitments. Therefore, in the future, it will be incumbent on us to provide settings where individuals will be granted the opportunity to increase their learning about living a contemplative life of prayer, spiritual direction, and soul care. This can be accomplished by offering sessions that uniquely embrace these disciplines. Such learning environments can be adopted in Sunday school, discipleship classes, or life groups (small groups).

The discipline of writing one's spiritual autobiography is needed in faith communities. Despite the vicissitudes of life that pull for one's attention, God desires that His people be in a maturing relationship with Him.

Caring for and nurturing the soul is one of the best gifts one can receive. Ultimately, the care of the soul is designed to bring glory to God. Regardless of tradition, denomination, ethnicity, economics, or class, God created His caring people to be in communion with Him and in community with one another.

Caring for the soul takes precious time. Unfortunately, living in a fast-paced, technologically advanced, social media–driven society, the tendency of some ministers, leaders, and individuals is to become inundated with activity. Consequently, there is less time for God and others. The practice of writing your spiritual autobiography is designed to give you permission to slow down and spend quality time with God as you reflect on His hand on your life.

Most of society is inundated with commitments that

pull us away from our primary relationship. Thus, your reflective writing will serve as a catalyst that will assist in bringing ministry leaders back to God, their first love.[1]

The vehicles of writing your spiritual autobiography will serve as the conduit that will prayerfully catapult you into a higher level of spiritual maturity in your life. Thus, the conclusion can be stated that this discipline will promote

- deepening a personal and more intimate relationship with God
- having a greater sensitivity to the presence of God
- transforming one's personal and public life
- developing a greater understanding of your spiritual journey
- being equipped and empowered to live out the resurrected life on a daily basis

Writing one's spiritual journey is a relatively new concept in many faith traditions; however, this book takes on enormous implications for furthering the teaching and the praxis of the discipline in faith communities and beyond.

My call is to serve the people of God. The clarion call is to minister to those God sends me to serve. It is to His glory that I go. Here I am, God; please send me,[2] your servant.

Fulfilled

Words cannot express how beneficial writing this book has been. At seventy-one years old, I continue to grow and mature in Christ. For some reason, we are programmed to think we have figured it all out by then, but not really. Every day is a new opportunity to learn about life.

While Gilbert and I were visiting Hilton Head, South

Carolina, for Christmas in 2024, we continued our weekly Tuesday and Thursday noonday devotion from the book *Jesus Calling* by Sarah Young. Many of us acknowledged that such a sacred learning space existed; however, when God woke me up at 3:30 a.m. on December 19, I knew there was some unfinished business that I needed to address. I began to pray, "Search me, God. One of my desires is to purchase fewer items. I believe You understand that."

When I was awakened, I began to question why I had purchased two sweatsuits and a sweatshirt the night before. In addition, on December 1, I had purchased some designer items. Yes, I knew it was near Christmas, but I did not need any of these items. This feeling was beyond living in a consumeristic society; the Spirit was trying to tell me something. I pressed in to hear. I cried out to know what was really going on. What was my internal void?

Immediately, my mind flashed back to the childhood days (from age ten to thirteen) I spent in Baltimore. As a little girl, I left home and went to live with Aunt Melba. During my stay there, I was blessed with nice things, but internally, I was missing my family in North Carolina. I was missing my parents, grandmother, siblings, cousins, and classmates. Until this point in my journey (while writing at this very moment), I never realized that there was an emptiness inside of me. And here I am, sixty-one years later, having this epiphany. In Baltimore, that emptiness was filled with my own room, toys, clothes, and the city life. That explains it. I had developed a habit of filling that space for over sixty years. I was filling a space that I never knew was void. I cried out, "Lord, heal me in the name of Jesus. Help me to return home." Like Dorothy, I, too, follow the yellow brick road. Like the wise men, I follow the star. It is not more clothes that I need. It is more of Jesus that I need. For as close as I sense I am to Him, there is a deeper closeness I have yet to find.

All of this is to say, in totality, we are all living out our childhood in some way. In what way are you trying to fill a void? Connect the dots!

This one moment fulfills the purpose of my writing the book. I am decreeing a shopping fast for 2025, and I pray beyond. I am filled in Him and do not need another thing.

Colossians 2:9–10 is our antidote. We are complete and filled in Christ. I am fulfilled.

APPENDIX 1

Teacher's Guide

Eight Christian education leaders in the Charlotte area said yes to the call. Our assignment was to write a comprehensive workbook for teachers in the faith community. One of the topics we emphasized was the discipline of prayer. Prayer cultivates the teacher's heart and is the key that unlocks the door to the heart of the students in the seats, both in person and online. Prayer is the key that unlocks hearts and minds so learning is more receptive and transformative. Prayer is the key that empowers teachers to make a difference in the lives of the learner.

As we embarked upon the journey of training teachers, God gave me a lovely prayer for teachers in the faith community to pray. It goes like this:

The Authoritative Teacher's Prayer

by Dr. Barbara Lewis Peacock

Most gracious God, I am so thankful that You called me out of darkness into the Marvelous Light.

I am in awe. You created me to be a teacher even before the foundation of the world. I thank You that You appointed me and You anointed me to teach the disciplined, the unruly, the believer and the unbeliever, the backslider, the drug addict and the prostitute, the whoremonger, the gossiper and the pimp, the young and the old, the rich and the poor, the black and the white.

I thank You that the teaching in me is not limited, for greater is He that is in me than He that is in the world.

I decree and declare that the lives of the students in my class will be transformed by the renewing of their minds, that they will know the good, the acceptable, and the perfect will of You.

I decree and declare, no weapon formed against me will prosper, and any tongue that rises against me will cease.

I pray a fresh anointing upon my students.

They are the head and not the tail.

They are blessed in their going out and their coming in.

They are blessed in the city and blessed in the country.

They are blessed in the marketplace and in the world.

They live by faith and not by sight.

They will enter into the classroom gates with thanksgiving. They will enter the courts of their seat with praise.

I commit to study to show myself approved unto God, a teacher that needs not be ashamed, for I will rightly divide the Word of Truth.

I commit to pray for each of my students and call them by their names.

I will love on my students.

I will build them up and not tear them down.

God, I thank You that You chose me and that You appointed me at this hour to penetrate the enemy of darkness.

I thank You that by faith my commitment to teach will make a difference throughout eternity.

It is in the precious and majestic name of Jesus Christ of Nazareth that I pray. Amen.[1]

I believe in the power of prayer and take each student God brings my way seriously. Therefore, I try to make it a habit to call out each student's name in prayer prior to our coming together. Teaching is a gift, a profession, and a vocational calling that should not be taken lightly. The book of James makes that very clear. He writes, "Not many of you should become teachers, my fellow believers, because you know that we who teach will be judged more strictly" (James 3:1).

In the book *Becoming Dallas Willard*, Gary Moon shares a song written by a blind man whose name is Ken Medema.[2] Though the song, "Teach Me to Stop and Listen," was written during an evening worship service at the Tilikum Retreat Center in Newberg, Oregon, Medema's song still speaks to us today. It reminds us to stop and listen, to slow down and sit in silence. It lifts up the importance of silence in discerning and centering ourselves.

It is out of the teacher's well of silence that love, truth, and transformation take place. The time we, as leaders, spend with God is irreplaceable. It is out of our warehouse of listening and silence that we are able to propel gestures of kindness to a world of hungry learners.

Encouragement

It always feels good to be encouraged. We live in a society where there is so much negativity. Teachers cannot read the minds of the students and thus do not have the capacity to know what is going on in each student's brain. Therefore, a word of encouragement is always in order to the learners.

Not every student will have a copy of this book. Therefore, please encourage them to purchase *Soul Journey: Transform Your Present by Rediscovering God in Your Past*. Even though you can teach a class to people with just the latter part of the book, which is the workbook, it is better for each student to have their own copy of the book.

Below are several suggested agendas based on the time-frame you choose to use the material.

Using material in a three- to five-hour workshop

- Teach the information found in chapter 8.
- After teaching, ask students to find a quiet space to write.
- Afterward, divide them into groups of three to six students to a facilitator (who has been trained prior to the breakouts).
- Instruct each student to share for ten to twenty minutes (based on what amount of time is conducive to the day).
- Each group should meet at the same time.
- Ask all groups to come back together as a large group.
- Encourage participants to continue examining their journey with a spiritual director.

Using material during a weekend retreat

- Teach the information found in chapter 8.
- After the teaching, ask students to write overnight.
- Afterward, divide them into groups of three to six students to a facilitator (who has been trained prior to the breakouts).
- Instruct each student to share for ten to twenty minutes (based on what amount of time is conducive to the day).
- Each group should meet at the same time.

- Ask all groups to come back together as a large group.
- Encourage participants to continue examining their journey with a spiritual director.

Planning an extended group study of a month or more

(This could be used prior to a cohort, a specified session, or a retreat.)

- Teach the information found in chapter 8.
- After the teaching, tell the students to go write on their own, and they will reconvene to discuss their spiritual autobiography at a later date.
- Give the students a month or more to seek the Holy Spirit for help with reflecting and writing.
- After their extended time away, reconvene.
- For groups of three to six, include a facilitator (who has been trained prior to the breakouts).
- Students come together in their group to share for ten to twenty minutes (based on what amount of time is conducive to the day).
- Each group meets at the same time.
- All groups come back together as a large group.
- Participants are encouraged to continue examining their journey with a spiritual director.

Once your sharing and document is completed, your journey is not over. Writing about your journey is a lifelong experience. It is good to go back periodically and update your writing as the Spirit continues to unveil His presence, direction, and power.

APPENDIX 2

A Covenant of Responsibility and Confidentiality

Below is a draft statement of Confidentiality for Peacock Soul Care. You will need to personalize it for your specific service, institution, and needs.

• • •

As a student of Peacock Soul Care or the spiritual autobiography group, I covenant to be responsible to my peers in this group by participating in the process. I will keep all discussions and interactions of this group **CONFIDENTIAL** and will not discuss them with anyone, other than the facilitators, without permission.

I understand that if I violate this covenant, it shall be a topic for discussion with the group. I also understand that any violation of this covenant, particularly with regard to violating the **CONFIDENTIALITY** of any or all members of this group, may result in my being dismissed from this group.

Participant's Printed Name Below:

Name ____

Date ____

Please note that teachers, intercessors, and facilitators are not operating in the position of a counselor or psychiatrist. If, during our discussion, it is noted that a life is at risk, it is the leader's responsibility to report such a case. If there is an expectation that a minor or elder is currently being abused or their life is at risk, it must be noted and reported.

We agree that the information you share about yourself will be held confidential.

Facilitator's Printed Name Below:

Name ____________________________________

Date ____________________________________

This confidentiality statement is entered into on this date, ____________________, with Barbara L. Peacock Ministries (BLP Ministries).

________________________________ {student's name} desires to have BLP Ministries perform the services of personal development referred to as a spiritual autobiography. BLP Ministries is willing to provide a safe space for encounters with God. Now, therefore, the parties hereby agree as follows:

BLP Ministries shall provide teaching on spiritual autobiography per the discussion. Please be mindful, BLP Ministries is not providing counseling or therapy of any kind.

Terms

BLP Ministries shall provide services during the period commencing on this date, ________________, and continuing through ________________.

Cancellations

BLP Ministries will require a minimum of twenty-four hours prior to a scheduled appointment for a cancellation from the client or organization.

Confidentiality

BLP Ministries and the student shall not disclose any proprietary or confidential information relating to the services provided to the client or class.

Ownership of Materials

Any materials or books prepared by Peacock Soul Care shall belong to and remain the property of the client. Peacock Soul Care may retain a copy of such documents for its records.

BLP Ministries shall be in receipt of your confidential spiritual autobiography on this date, ______________________.

____ ____________

Facilitator signature Date

____ ____________

Student signature Date

Email ____

Phone ____

APPENDIX 3

Creative Expression of a Spiritual Autobiography Through Quilting Practices

The section below is from the spiritual formation class of cohort 2 of the institute, Peacock Soul Care. The students are:

- Annette Gathers
- Mary Hellberg
- Greta Jones
- Sandy Robinson
- Gwen Smith
- Sheila Tolan

Woven by the Master

That's why we can be so sure that every detail in our lives of love for God is worked into something good. God knew what he was doing from the very beginning. He decided from the outset to shape the lives of those who love him along the same lines as the life of his Son.

Romans 8:28–29 MSG

Introduction and History

A quilt is composed of materials from various places. A quilt is made up of more than scraps of fabric that are stitched together. Quilts have a major purpose in that they provide a unique god-given story. Over centuries, quilts have shared journeys in various cultures. They can express what words cannot. In a quilt, each piece of fabric finds its place. Like a written spiritual autobiography, quilts have a multiplicity of pieces, twists, and turns.

Think about some of your old clothing. Your favorite blanket or a favorite dress. Independently, they are just old items, but when you put them together, they make up an amazing tapestry. On their own, they seem insignificant and worn, but when you put them together, they tell a story. In the hands of a quilt maker, they become part of a beautiful design. The same is true of our independent lives. Our struggles, pains, and triumphs—every piece of our stories—are not wasted. God, the Master Quilter, uses each stitch and each piece to weave a purpose far greater than what we can imagine.

During slavery, quilts had many meaningful functions. They warmed men, women, and children on brutally cold nights. In addition, quilts sometimes carried trusted messages of hope and freedom. Women who were slaves were known to put together pieces of fabric to make a quilt. Often, they were not just creating an item for keeping someone warm, they were stitching together a sacred message.

As we look at our individual stories, we may not understand all the broken pieces. We may have questions like:

- Why so much pain?
- Was God there?
- Why did my loved one die?
- Why this sickness?

However, when we surrender everything to God and seek His divine plan, the scattered scraps, pain, and tears of our life, when put together, begin to make a story. Putting the pieces of fabric together is a holistic reminder that God was faithful to work it all together for good (Romans 8:28). When we tell our own stories and trust God with the messy, incomplete pieces of our lives, we become living quilts, sewn together by His love.

So, as you look at the scraps, the fringes, and the patches of your life, be encouraged. Even when the design seems foggy and challenging to comprehend, God was there. When the colors seem mismatched, just remember that God, the Master Quilter, is always putting the pieces together. Through the Holy Spirit, God divinely stitches every thread and every moment into a tapestry of love and hope. When it is all said and done, you will see such a beautifully quilted life!

APPENDIX 4

Abbreviated Spiritual Autobiography Journey

- Begin your spiritual autobiography bathed in prayer.
- Practice breathing exercises. Breathe in through your nose, hold for four seconds, and then blow out your mouth for four seconds.
- Read slowly Psalm 139:13–18 NKJV. Identify one word that stands out to you. Then read Psalm 139:13–18 MSG. Identify one word that stands out to you. Ponder those words and what they mean to you.
- Look into your mirror and begin to assess the inner layers of your being.
- Answer the following questions:

    Who do you see?
    What do you see?
    How do you feel?

  Sit in those answers for a moment.
- Beginning the creative process, use the decades of your life to help you get started. For example:

    0–10 years
    11–20 years

21–30 years

31–40 years

41–50 years

51–60 years, etc.

- Then use these questions to help you begin writing or putting your creative thoughts together.

    Who were the most important people in my life?

    What was the most memorable moment?

    How did I see myself?

    What was my most pivotal moment?

    What was the most important decision I made?

    I experienced a crisis of belief when ____________ because ____________.

    Go deeper and answer why to each question above.

- Examples of materials you may want to use.

    Colored or plain paper, index cards, cardstock, magazine, notebook cover, or Post-it notes

    Crayons, markers, glue sticks, single or double-sided tape, rulers

    Colored yarn, thread, canvas

    Journals and pens

    Picture frames (optional, for finished work)

    Material or fabric that holds personal meaning, remnants from a loved one, etc.

    Pictures or photos to highlight your journey

    Scripture(s) or event(s) from your spiritual autobiography

    Scissors to cut things apart

    Seam ripper to break and remove lines of stitching that went wrong

Needle to guide the thread to stitch a pattern
Thread to weave things together
Pin(s to hold things in place
Rotary cutter to cut fabric
Self-healing cutting mat to protect table tops when cutting. It heals after being cut on.

- Personalize by naming your quilt!

NOTES

Introduction

1. Jessica Kendall Ingram, *A Journey in the Experience of Prayer* (Journey Press, 2006), 3.
2. "Therefore go and make disciples of all nations, baptizing them in the name of the Father and of the Son and of the Holy Spirit" (Matthew 28:19).

Chapter 1—The Before

1. The Greek word for pericope is *perikope*. Pericope simply refers to a section of Scripture. It includes a beginning, middle, and an end. A pericope captures a full teaching or thought in a biblical passage.
2. Jeremiah 1:5.
3. James Weldon Johnson, *God's Trombones* (Viking Press, Inc., 1927).
4. James Luther Mays, *Psalms, Interpretation: A Bible Commentary for Teaching and Preaching* (John Knox Press, 1994), 426.
5. Mays, *Psalms*, 428.
6. "I love those who love me, and those who seek me find me" (Proverbs 8:17).
7. Dallas Willard, *Hearing God* (Renovate Institute, 2011) as quoted in Gary Moon, *Becoming Dallas Willard:*

The Formation of a Philosopher, Teacher, and Christ Follower (InterVarsity Press, 2018), 35.

Chapter 2—Dear Diary

1. Donnie McClurkin, "Church Medley" https://www.youtube.com/watch?v=Txt42RN9pWs.

Chapter 3—A Spiritual Autobiography

1. Henri J. M. Nouwen, *The Genesee Diary: Report from a Trappist Monastery* (Doubleday, 1976), 19–20.
2. Maya Angelou, *Wouldn't Take Nothing for My Journey Now* (Random House, 1993), 12.

Chapter 4—Biblical Foundation for a Spiritual Autobiography

1. "Then God said, 'Let us make mankind in our image, in our likeness, so that they may rule over the fish in the sea and the birds in the sky, over the livestock and all the wild animals, and over all the creatures that move along the ground.' So God created mankind in his own image, in the image of God he created them; male and female he created them. God blessed them and said to them, 'Be fruitful and increase in number; fill the earth and subdue it. Rule over the fish in the sea and the birds in the sky and over every living creature that moves on the ground'" (Genesis 1:26–28).
2. "Doctrines—Life Helps," in *Disciple's Study Bible: New International Version*, (Cornerstone Bible Publishers, 1984), 3.
3. "Apostle's Creed," African Methodist Episcopal Church, accessed December 2, 2024, https://www.ame-church.com/our-church/our-beliefs/.
4. Description for *An Autobiography of a Person in the*

Spirit by Witness Lee, (Living Stream Ministry, 2024) found at https://www.livingstream.com/en/life/7002001-autobiography-of-a-person-in-the-spirit-an.html.

Chapter 5—History of a Spiritual Autobiography

1. Elizabeth Powers and Amy Mandelker, eds., *Pilgrim Souls: A Collection of Spiritual Autobiography*, introduction by Madeleine L'Engle (Touchstone, 1999), 16.
2. Augustine, *Confessions*, trans. R. S. Pine-Coffin (Penguin Books, 1961), 11.
3. Augustine, *Confessions*, 28.
4. Volker Henning Drecoll, "Grace," in *The Cambridge Companion to Augustine's Confessions*, ed. Tarmo Toom (Cambridge University Press, 2020), 107–22.
5. John Bunyan, *Grace Abounding to the Chief of Sinners—Updated Edition: A Brief Account of God's Exceeding Mercy Through Christ to His Poor Servant*, John Bunyan, ed. P. Miller (Aneko Press, 2018), 20.
6. Ephesians 3:20.
7. "For our struggle is not against flesh and blood, but against the rulers, against the authorities, against the powers of this dark world and against the spiritual forces of evil in the heavenly realms" (Ephesians 6:12).
8. Carmelite is a Roman Catholic religious order that originated in the 12th century. Spiritual focus and core disciplines include loving others, contemplating, praying, detaching, and simplicity.
9. Howard Thurman, *With Head and Heart: The Autobiography of Howard Thurman* (Harcourt Brace Jovanovich, 1979).
10. Kathleen Lynch, "Protestant Autobiography in the Seventeenth-Century Anglophone World, Conversion Narratives in Early Modern Europe," August 29, 2012,

https://europeanconversionnarratives.wordpress.com/2012/08/29/kathleen-lynch-protestant-autobiography-in-the-seventeenth-century-anglophone-world/.

Chapter 6—The Epiphany of Seeing the Star

1. Brother Lawrence, *The Practice of the Presence of God the Best Rule of a Holy Life: Being Conversations and Letters of Nicholas Herman of Lorraine (Brother Lawrence),* trans. Joseph de Beaufort (F. H. Revell Company, 1895).
2. Jan Richardson, *Circle of Grace: A Book of Blessings for the Seasons* (Orlando: Wanton Gospeller Press, 2015), 71. Used with permission.

Chapter 7—Your Eschatological Life

1. Dallas Willard, *Renovation of the Heart: Putting on the Character of Christ* (NavPress, 2002), 122. Quoted in *Becoming Dallas Willard: The Formation of a Philosopher, Teacher, and Christ Follower* (InterVarsity Press, 2018), 148.
2. Augustine, *Confessions*, 263.
3. Barbara L Peacock, "The Days of Our Lives," The Park Church, Charlotte, North Carolina, 2019.
4. To read all lyrics to this song, go to https://www.allgospellyrics.com/index.php?sec=listing&lyricid=1346.

Chapter 8—Spiritual Autobiography Workbook

1. Our website, www.peacocksoulcare.com, has several directors you can choose from. If you need any assistance, please do not hesitate to reach out to us.
2. To learn more about writing your spiritual autobiography with Peacock Soul Care (www

.peacocksoulcare.com), please go to our website to see the days that we will be offering the course online.
3. Richard Peace, *Spiritual Autobiography: Discovering and Sharing Your Spiritual Story* (Navpress, 1998), 11.
4. Peace, *Spiritual Autobiography*, 88.
5. Augustine, *Confessions*, 214.

Conclusion

1. 1 John 4:7–16.
2. Matthew 28:18–20.

Appendix 1: Teacher's Guide

1. Barbara L. Peacock, "The Authoritative Teacher's Prayer," 2013. Used with permission from author.
2. Gary Moon, *Becoming Dallas Willard*, quotes from Ken Medema, "Teach me to Stop and Listen" (Word Music, 1978).

Special thanks to my family: Vérnee Peacock Wilkinson (right), Michael Wilkinson (center), Eden, and Eliah (far left).

And of course, my husband, Gilbert.

See Us.

Hear Us.

Experience VOICES.

VOICES amplifies the strengths, struggles, and courageous faith of Black image bearers of God.

Podcasts, blogs, books, films, and more . . .

Find out more at **experiencevoices.org**

Spread the Word by Doing One Thing.

- Give a copy of this book as a gift.
- Share the QR code link via your social media.
- Write a review of this book on your blog, favorite bookseller's website, or at ourdailybreadpublishing.org.
- Recommend this book to your church, small group, or book club.

Connect with us.

Our Daily Bread Publishing
PO Box 3566, Grand Rapids, MI 49501, USA
Email: books@odbm.org

Love God. Love Others.

with Our Daily Bread®

Your gift changes lives.

Connect with us.

Our Daily Bread Publishing
PO Box 3566, Grand Rapids, MI 49501, USA
Email: books@odbm.org